THE MARKET

THE MARKET

CRYPTO WALL STREET

YOLANDA C. RONDON

NEW DEGREE PRESS

THE MARKET

Crypto Wall Street

ISBN

978-1-64137-367-8   *Paperback*

978-1-64137-714-0   *Ebook*

I dedicate this book to my grandma who watched this little girl climb up the red sofa in the South Bronx.

My grandma and I laugh at Sophia and Rose on television. I do not fall. I take my place right by your side. You go through your purse and looking for a peppermint or cough drop to give me. I, this little girl looks up at you, with her big bright brown eyes. It's only me grandma, don't worry, I made it.

CONTENTS

INTRODUCTION

———

Technology is a blessing. It is also a curse.

Perhaps that's the tension between the speed of innovation and evolution. Some good; some bad, nothing is clear.

Depending on your perspective, you may think society has blossomed, I would say much of the developing world may agree, but not necessarily in a good way. But true financial equal access and access to opportunity remain out of reach for the people. You may be happy with the ability to search for a new home with a tap on your phone or shop for your groceries from your bed with the push of the button. But this reflects a society that wants things just to have them and wants them now. This may be just for a matter of convenience but for people around the world, food and shelter is a matter of efficiency and need.

Technology has allowed people all over the world to be able to connect with one another, but the reality is that technology has blocked actual in-person relationships, where people are alone obsessing over their phones, seeking online affirmation of who they are. In a world that is increasingly more connected through technology, people are deprived of human connections more than ever and the connections they do have are not real.

Technology can be used to address many social, economic, and humanitarian issues. Imagine aid being delivered directly to the mother struggling to get formula for her newborn baby in a humanitarian crisis. Think about how much drinking water your donation could actually support, if there were no transaction fees and no hands dipping into the pot. What about communities receiving development grants? We can stop a lot of the corruption by closing the multiple layers that aid must flow through. Whole communities of the unbanked population estimated as high as two billion people, now with access to enter the market space, develop businesses, and grow independent self-sustaining economies separate from banks and the government.

Often the people have looked to those in power for help—the institutions, the banks, and the government. Those directly or indirectly responsible for their plight—by their actions that seek profit, that support the chains of capitalism, and fail to act to stop exploitation, fraud, and manipulation—the disenfranchised seek answers.

Communities should be educated on how cryptocurrency works and empowered through self-sustaining programs like microfinance initiatives that have low interest and provide management and advice. There may be places where internet access is restricted or monitored, but innovation is steadfast in overcoming these hurdles. An exemplary innovation is the Tor browser that enables use of the internet anonymously, enabling the security of users who fear government actors monitoring their speech, and their use of the internet dangers their lives.

Most past and current attempts to utilize technology to help disenfranchised communities and communities of color are inadequate. Often, they reflect short-term initiatives or projects that limit access, which cannot sustain long term impact or scalability.

> *"Everyone wants to be seen making a difference*
> *but no one wants to actually make a change."*

But there is a shift occurring. In the backdrop of the rise of protests and the Occupy Wall Street movement, financial crises and demands for change across the world, the people are taking action. They understand that they are more powerful together, and they can create the change they seek. We the people are so intertwined and connected throughout the world, partly thanks to technology, we are eerily codependent. The people are flipping the system on its head. First it was the computer, then it was the internet, and now its cryptocurrency and blockchain technology.

So, what is cryptocurrency?

Cryptocurrency is a digital currency that operates online. It is independent of a central bank and uses encryption techniques to self-regulate the currency and verify the transfer of funds. Cryptocurrency relies on block-chain technology.

Blockchain technology is a peer to peer network that operates online. It uses a distributed ledger with built-in authentication of transaction and record keeping, which cannot be changed. The blockchain verifies each transaction through the unique assignment of hashes to each Bitcoin from each prior transaction since the Bitcoin's creation. Each transaction builds on another to build the blockchain that must be verified to ensure ownership of the bitcoin by the spender. There are no fees to transfer Bitcoin within minutes anywhere in the world to anyone with access to the internet. The blockchain is secure and Bitcoin's blockchain is practically unable to hack.

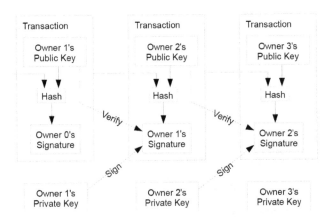

Transactions Diagram from the 2008 White Paper, Bitcoin: A Peer-to-Peer Electronic Cash System. Source: bitcoin.org/bitcoin.pdf

No one knows who created Bitcoin, the first crypto-currency. In 2008, a paper entitled "Bitcoin: A Peer-to-Peer Electronic Cash System" was posted to a mailing list discussion on cryptography by Satoshi Nakamoto. The real identity of Satoshi Nakamoto remains a mystery to this day. Bitcoin emerged on the internet in 2009 with the Bitcoin software made publicly available and changed the course of our future. Everyone was talking about it. At first it was just gossip and those who were investing in it, were told they were crazy fools and it was a Ponzi scheme. But people started making money and then everyone wanted to get in on it. The noise began to shake the financial industry.In 2010, 10,000 bitcoins were exchanged for two pizzas. Before 2010, the exact value of Bitcoin was not known. From there, there were copycats of the Bitcoin design created and various versions of cryptocurrency like tokens emerged. In 2013, the value of Bitcoin fell from a value high of $266 and many lost money with the shutdown of Silk Road, a marketplace that used Bitcoin. Scammers painted a dark cloud over Bitcoin, with bitcoin owners of 850,000 bitcoins being scammed out of nearly $450 million by the bitcoin exchange, Mt. Gox, in 2014. But the market value of Bitcoin rose again. By the end of 2017, Bitcoin jumped from the value of $11,500 to nearly $20,000. In 2018, the Bitcoin market crashed, and this time around, people lost billions.

Just like any market, cryptocurrency is subject to fluctuations of the marketplace. But people were blinded by the excitement of all the money. The value of Bitcoin kept going up and up and took on a life of its own. The feeling was that you could not lose, it was practically free money. But Bitcoin was not invisible to market forces, and amid all the hype on all the self-made millionaires and frivolous spending, there was not much education or news coverage on the risks and fiscal responsibility.

At the same time, there were efforts to use crypto for good. Cryptocurrency helps women in Afghanistan, who are not allowed to open bank accounts, to get paid in bitcoin for their work. This is, of course, empowering women to enter the workforce and develop their own businesses. The use of cryptocurrency to help humanitarian efforts through digital donations has also supported bringing rapid relief to impacted communities quickly.

Today, there are over a thousand variations of cryptocurrencies that exist within the market, but the original Bitcoin design remains the underlying foundation for all. There are merely additions made to the coding to improve on the speed, security, or anonymity. Innovation and the accessibility to use Bitcoin on more platforms, has increased its mass appeal beyond computer coders to cross generational familiarity and popularity. With cryptocurrency exchanges and crypto wallets, and initial coin offerings, the industry is innovating and will continue to do so.

The mystery that surrounds the origins of cryptocurrency are intriguing, as to understanding the purpose and the civil liberties principles behind the emerging economy. Especially when bad actors (not only those on the darknet) want to use and exploit it, and capitalists are out to destroy it.

The true power of Bitcoin lies in blockchain technology. Crypto and blockchain technology may be a tool to help break many barriers, but will it help anyone? The government agencies and politicians have an opinion. They demand regulation on a decentralized online economy independent from the government that protects privacy. The corporations and banks are panicking because for once they are cut off from their exploitative fees.

The crypto economy and network are powered by the people for the people. The network literally cannot function without people contributing their time, energy, and computers to verify transactions in the economy.

Welcome to the market

And with it: the good and the bad.

PART I

"*Today, the most efficient way to get money to London is to buy an airplane ticket and take it there myself. I can stream video from the space station but cannot move my money from point A to point B efficiently.*"

—RIPPLE LABS CEO, BRAD GARLINGHOUSE

CHAPTER 1

THE PROPOSAL

———

Sam had a long day at work, it seemed like it would never end. Taking over the family farm was decided by virtue of his birth, but tough, nevertheless. Sam went to school for accounting, a somewhat different life than trudging through rows of strawberries and stacking strawberries for sale. His parents, grandparents, great grandparents, and their parents before them have always grown strawberries. It was their livelihood.

His father began teaching Sam how to grow strawberries from a very young age. Sam learned the role of growing strawberries from the care of the soil to the business side of selling the strawberries and negotiating deals. It was important, as well as a sense of pride, for his son to understand every facet of the farm. Sam's father worked to develop and grow the farm adding a 1/4 acre to the original plot of farmland. He even opened an office in town to market their strawberries to a wider audience.

As his parents got older, it was natural that Sam would increasingly take on more responsibility despite being in school full time and working on the farm during the summer and spring breaks. While his classmates and friends were gaining internship experience, extra cash from summer gigs, or a tan at the beach, Sam was on his feet twelve hours a day with the sun beaming on his back and shoulders. Sam applied his accounting skills to the farm, producing data and analysis to maximize efficiency, growth, and quality. Sam truly did not mind helping his folks.

Even today, he missed the warm summer nights spent with his mother lying on the grass, looking up at the clear crisp sky, counting the stars, and identifying the constellations that the stars made in the sky. This was the time he would share his ideas, reserving his questions and witty comments from what he may have saw in town or overheard for this time under the stars with a cup of strawberries plucked that day.

Sam valued the patience and tenderness his mother exuded. She was always encouraging him to speak freely and encouraging his inquisitive mind. While his father always thought Sam should work more and talk less, as he believed a man must be a man of action, his father did not stifle his questioning nature. When Sam entered his adolescent years, his father helped him discover an outlet to redirect some of that energy: chess.

Chess allowed him the questioning of his opponents' strategy and motives for each action while also leaving Sam to calculate his opponent's moves in advance and the probability of his opponents' actions to ultimately enable Sam to win. Shaping him into who Sam is, chess developed his keen eye for detail and emboldened his questioning nature which was ever present today. It came in handy as an accountant, not only for the family farm, but when providing auditing services to other neighboring farms for tax purposes. Today, Sam also led a collective of family farmers and had doubled his family's market share in the strawberry market. Sam supplied beyond just grocery stores and restaurants, he also supplied to natural beauty products and internet-based meal prep companies.

* * *

It's been a while—well, more than a while—months since Sam spent time with his college friends. The responsibility of the farm kept him quite busy and he did not get into the city too often. But he did enjoy a change of scenery every now and then. He rents an apartment downtown allowing him the flexibility to split his time at the business office and on the farm itself to handle operations. Game night is a great reason to invite everyone over for drinks and catch up with everything going on. All the classic games are there: Uno, Dominoes, Jenga, and Monopoly.

Sam went out and made sure to stock up on their favorite local craft beer and grabbed a bottle of Jack too. Sam even set up his DVR with some pointedly political comedy commentary. That will get them through the appetizers and first course.

Sam hears someone clearing their throat. Stepping away from the stove, Sam walks around the kitchen island toward the living room. Sam sees Brad, he is sitting on the couch, but even sitting, he looked like a giant. He sat casually with his back and shoulders straight and legs crossed. He generally kept to himself but a jokester among those whom he allowed to be in his company. A unique humor most would say, and his jokes would always have a twinge of political undertone, appealing to the sarcastic personality type.

"I see you still, um ... choking on that privilege," said Brad.

Sam recognizes the voice, followed by a long drawl to substitute for a number of "ums" in any sentence, anywhere. Brad's semi-awkward dry joke makes him smile. He commands attention everywhere he goes and even now, looming down on Sam from the couch.

Sam met Brad in college, at Berkeley. Brad was Sam's Spanish language tutor. Sam went from a C on his Spanish midterm to a B+. Not bad, although Sam would barely be able to ask for food in Spanish today. Self-taught, Sam did not know how Brad learned to speak Spanish, as there was not an ounce of Spanish in his background.

He vividly remembers Brad's speech at graduation to the student body. His speech was more than the generic message that you could do anything you set your mind to. It was deeper than that. He told us that the degree is not important. That our value to society was more than what could be measured by the eye and they should strive to add value to society not simply be successful. Brad always applied the same principled determination and studious nature from his academic life to his personal life, too. The air around him always made everyone feel better.

Back then, Brad was exactly what you pictured when you think of a lawyer. He participated in all the political clubs and even served on the debate team. Always busy doing everything. Sam knew Brad even ran for student government, but he didn't win. Which is pretty much the only time Brad hadn't gotten what he wanted in life. Student government was more of a popularity contest, anyway.

Sam remembers when he and Brad were assigned a team presentation together in history class. Brad had made several attempts to schedule time with Sam to complete the team assignment and prepare for the presentation. But Sam would either not show up or show up barely functioning. Moto is to blame for most of it. Sam was probably out with him getting hammered. Sam did show up for the actual presentation. Brad explained to the class that Sam had put together the poster board, so he would primarily speak. Sam was shocked and even more so when Brad took the professor aside after to class to explain that he had done all the work on the project and had complied meticulous notes to prove it. Sam respected Brad for it. Brad wanted to make sure that credit was given where it was due, clearly all to him. But because they were a team, it was none of the other students' business what happened or did not happen. Sam failed that project and nearly failed the class but gained a lifelong friend.

Brad is an avid planner and puts serious energy and thought into the woman he fancied. Like any romantic interest, a person may find out what they liked to do, where they were from, and even their favorite food. But Brad approaches his romantic life with intent of assessing compatibility with ambition. Planning out his life since the age of twelve, any woman Brad likes must have a plan too. By the time Brad turned twenty years old he graduated from college and by twenty-three he received his Juris Doctorate. At twenty-four years old, Brad became a licensed attorney and from twenty-four to thirty he worked at a firm gaining experience and connections. Most importantly, Brad was paying off any student loan debt. With that out of the way by thirty years old, he is a public interest lawyer, working in under-served communities and offering pro bono legal representation. This is exactly what Brad did and then some.

The author of several peer review journal articles, research and a textbook contributor, Brad by all means, is successful. But more importantly, he is adding value back into the community. Brad owns his own firm in an under-developed area of Los Angeles. He made it a point to invest in neighboring businesses around his firm, to help uplift the surrounding areas. He leads mentoring programs geared toward encouraging public interest and in the LA inner city youth. Through his firm, beyond his public interest litigation work, he also serves as a policy consultant, appellate brief writer, and an anti-corruption and record keeping attorney to major companies. Brad is a jack of all trades, running his own firm just like he planned. He is still figuring out the romantic side, but as he said he would rather get the right wife the first time.

"Just come on in Brad, make yourself comfortable." Sam smirks.

"I did and I'm good," states Brad like an unquestionable fact as he kicks his feet up on the coffee table. "You don't lock your door?"

Looking at Brad, Sam can tell he is bald by choice. He has some facial hair just over his mouth and patches on his jaw line with a stern commanding voice and firm handshake.

"For what, nobody is going to come in here and take anything. You can close the door if you like, but you don't need to lock it," Sam said.

"You need any help with anything?" Brad asks.

"I got everything under control," Sam responds.

"Sam, when is everybody else arriving?"

"They're supposed to be here now. But I expect them to trickle in little by little. Moto is coming over, too. He asked me about using my printer to make some copies, which means that we are going to hear one of Moto's investment opportunity presentations tonight." Sam has sat through a Moto elevator pitch before and his fair share of "This is great, but do not think this investment is for me?" conversations.

Sam misses the good old days—Moto and everyone. To be twenty something again, oh he wishes. But he knows that other factors weigh on their life choices, the considerations that come with age, sobriety, and bills. The consequences of adulthood and all the responsibility that came with it definitely put a damper on his life's expectations. But Sam always likes to be certain of things. No action taken without serious thought on what the fall out could be. His friends always made fun of him for playing it too safe, that he would forget to enjoy life. Money is not a problem, but he did not spend any. Any money spent is money that he can save. The question was: what was he exactly saving it for?

"We had some good times, Brad."

"I know, Sam. Remember that time we went to jail out in Berkeley, California?"

"Oh no, do not remind me. That was still your entire fault, Brad."

"Nope, this is communal blame. We are all guilty by association."

Sam and Brad laugh.

"I still say that those police officers violated our right to freedom of speech and expression," Sam stated.

Brad gives Sam a look. His head cocks to the side, raising his eyebrows. He begins the inquisition.

"Really Sam, you printed poster-board sized pictures of the school administrators' private emails and then put them up all over school property! I think maybe you went just a little too far."

"But remember, those emails revealed that the school was mishandling our tuition payments and went into debt," Sam responded. "That they tried to get out of debt by gambling with our tuition fees and selling our data from our internet usage on school computers and school network to private companies. And when that did not work, they got in cahoots with that bank."

They were frauds and someone had to call them out on it. And it just happened to be Sam.

"Brad, now you're trying to say the posters and the protests, just happened huh?" Sam asks.

Brad shakes his head, "How did you get those emails anyway?"

"I always protect my sources." Sam responds.

Brad shakes his head.

Sam continues, "Berkeley, just stuck up though."

"Okay, Sam. Is this what we are going with now?" Brad asks.

"Yes, that is my story and I'm sticking to it." Sam says with a laugh.

bbbzzz. The door buzzer sounds.

"Brad, can you get the door for me? Just hit the button on the intercom."

"Who is it?"

"It's Moto and Lars."

"Hey, come on up," Brad said into the intercom.

- bbbzzz -

From downstairs, Lars yells, "I come bearing gifts!"

Step. Step. Creak. Step. Step. Creak. Step. Step. Step. Step.

"Its 2008, how do you not have an elevator?"

"It's only two flights, Lars. Stop being lazy," said Moto. "I like the decor and interior design of the building, it has character. An elevator would ruin that."

The building was quite beautiful. From the outside, the building looked like your run of the mill luxury building with a glass and brick finish. Only fob key access to the building. Nice trimmed hedges entering the building, passing by the security guard, and the beauty of the building is a surprise, like entering a different time and place. You cannot tell from the outside that the building possessed the archways and the details in the sculpting of the crown moldings. So unique were the chandeliers.

As Lars walks up the first flight of stairs, her hands curved around with the banister leading up to the next flight of stairs. "Bannister's, commonly known as handrails now, no longer curve or connect to each other, they just stop. Ah, the little things."

Step. Creak. Step. Creak. Step. Step. Step. Step. Step. Step.

"We got good old-fashioned Moonshine for you Sam!" exclaims Lars. "The heart of America! I hope you enjoy it."

"We will. Thank you, Lars."

"And I do not know this guy behind me. I met this stranger on the train, like a lost puppy."

Everyone laughs.

"No, I'm serious. I almost did not recognize him under all that hair. Moto, you need a haircut."

Moto brushed his shaggy black hair out of his face and racked his left hand through his hair before removing his glasses revealing the face of a man in his mid-thirties with rugged features. Hidden behind his motorcycle shades were light dark baggy eyes.

Lars couldn't believe it when she ran into Moto in route to Sam's house. She saw this guy on the BART reading. And not just any old book, but a book titled, "Human Capital. Uncle Sam owns you!" Picture it. A figure sitting on the train with this book open, where the man standing in front of him holding on to the pole in a suit with his tie loosened around his neck, fumbles with his newspaper, "The Wall Street Journal." The woman sitting right next to him is breaking the packaging to her new iPod and the passengers directly across from him on his left are arguing about the impact of the raise in minimum wage on small businesses. All the conflicting vibes Lars was getting from that scene, so of course she had to approach the guy. Lars could not really see the guy from where he was standing by the car door because of all the hair in his face. But as she approached the guy with the book, she realized it was Moto. Only he would read some book like that on the train, always there to stir up controversy, just like in college.

"It has been a long time. Where is Sean? Have you heard from him?" Lars asks the group.

"He is always traveling for work. He told me he was coming but he didn't respond to my morning reminder text I sent to everyone in the group," Brad responds.

Everyone grabs a bar stool from around the kitchen island to eat together. The dining table is too formal and eating in the living room on the couches separates everyone into mini side conversations. At the kitchen island they can all be together.

"Sam, what's new?" Lars asks.

"Just working, same old same old. Trying to take the family on vacation to Hawaii, we need to get away for a little while. We have not been able to go anywhere in quite a while. We took a hit with the economic downturn. I mean we all struggled; I know. We survived but children are expensive…"

"Hmm…I need a drink." Lars giggles.

* * *

From inside his Camry, Joe watches outside Sam's front room window. The blue window curtains were partially drawn, but the window was open. Peering through the window he could see the living room. This was the only lit up window on the street. He imagined the laughter and conversations. It was like a separate haven from the outside world, filled with music. The light seemed to dance on their faces, as they lit up with joy from every joke followed by a drink and dinging their glasses together for toasts.

The conversation seems to get more intense, as a person with just hair enters the scene. Joe cannot see his face, only the person's hands coming out of the long sleeve black shirt. The person makes motions with his hands as their mouth moves. Who is this strange figure in the apartment? Does he know him? He wants to find out.

He receives a text asking for his ETA. Looking back at the window, he clicks the phone on to the clip on to the right side of his jeans. He grabs the car door handle, catching a glimpse of himself in the rear-view mirror. He hesitates and stops short of pushing the car door open.

A part of him wants to remain the car. Out of sight and out of the range of inquisitions on his life from familiar strangers. He really enjoys his own solace and wishes to just be left alone. But he takes a deep breath, places his left foot on the ground. Finally, he pushes the intercom buttons to Sam's apartment.

bbzz.

He passes the security guard, through the archway with crown moldings, up two flights of steps to the home of the only window lit up on the street.

"Oh, here comes the prodigal son," Brad quips.

"Here we go, Brad. I am well, how are you?" replies Joe.

"Uncomfortable debates and drinks, what more can I ask for?"

"You would say that, Brad!" Lars says between bites.

"Pass that moonshine," Brad states while reaching for the bottle.

"Since you guys are letting go of your inhibitions and I got you under the influence of the libations, I want to discuss a proposal with you guys." states Moto.

Ahh. "Oh, here we go. No Ponzi schemes today, Moto."

Moto continues, "You know, there is a shift in how people view governments and its role. People all over the world no longer want to be dependent upon corrupt governments to survive, to change their lives and lives of their heirs, and make a difference. Just the other day, the city newspaper published a report after a six-month investigation that detailed with documents to support its finding that it is always the same few people at the top, identifying them by name across industries and political campaign finance etc. The wealth stays in that tiny circle of the one percent and this is by design."

"Sorry to interrupt your annual mid-life crisis, Moto," Joe begins. "But this is always how it has been and likely how it always will be for the foreseeable future. It does not matter. There is no point in dwelling on something that we cannot change. Money is not going to solve all our problems anyway. All you can do is try your best and live your life. Being part of the one percent is the end goal or the only route to happiness.

Let's be frank, most wealthy people are just as miserable as us. We think they have all this money and they should have no problems. They create problems, I just don't get it."

"Joe is right," Lars adds. "Look no further than the SAT scandal, with the rich bribing proctors to doctor their children's exams."

Joe nods and he picks up where Lars left off. "There was no need. The children of the rich have nearly every opportunity and access to succeed because they have the wealth and connections. They just don't want to work hard, and they raise their children with no character, no purpose, and being selfish. They run around the world oblivious. The fact that the world does not care about whom they are, their feelings, and what they want. Little do they know; they don't deserve anything, and their entitlement and greed is common."

Lars states, "I hear you. People got nothing better to do with their lives than to get over it. Despite every advantage and opportunity, they have, they just want more and more. I had to scrape my pennies and work three jobs during summer break, just to have barely enough to get by during the school year."

"I remember that summer you got the model gig, Sam." Joe sucks his teeth, trying to recall the name of the job. "What was it again? I want to get this right. It was that local beach California wannabe surfer boy store. All I know is that they sold the same shit with their name all over everything in different colors. Like I forgot where I bought my clothes. And that cologne could kill you on contact. I walk in the store, and that cologne is sprayed like there are timed sensors, so strong I can taste it. And that would be it. Walk straight out."

"It was not that bad, and I learned a lot about communication and salesmanship," replies Sam.

"Listen here, you want to make someone else rich, go right ahead. Like a walking Cali beach boy advertisement. Yeah, that is what you were. That cologne gave me headaches. And you thought you were going to make it as a model for real." Lars laughs. "Then he saw that check for like $300."

"That was straight robbery!" exclaims Sam.

"That was back when minimum wage was what? $5.15, though right?!" states Brad.

"They took half my paycheck from me. I mean, they still do. The more I make, the more they take. Fed tax, state tax, local tax, county tax, tax, tax, tax. Like damn!" Sam exclaims.

Moto interjects.

"Imagine a world where you do not have to pay Uncle Sam for the money you earned. They waste the money they take out in our taxes! I know I do not see even half of where my tax money actually goes to and is used correctly to better society, other than making some politician rich to sit on his ass all day and do nothing - but making grand gestures and speeches but no substance or actual action! I don't know about you, but I am fed up with the excuses and taking all my money!"

Pointing to everyone in the room Moto continues, "We can reinvent what it means to be wealthy and how to create wealth. To breathe new life into the American Dream! We know what we have to do to create this world and we must flip the system on its head!"

Moto takes a step back, looking in the eye of every person in the room individually. "If we think creatively, we can maximize our potential through an interconnected and growing dependent world and solely independent currency, digital currency that can be used by anyone, anywhere and truly by the people, for the people!"

"No smart comments from you, Brad?" Lars joked.

Brad sighed. "Well since you asked. I would say that it sounds nice. But what is the exact good or service we are selling, and like many great ideas that fail, what is the execution plan?"

Moto responds at length.

"Many people think that with technology, the work performed by the human beings will become obsolete and/or counterproductive to cost-efficiency. While this may be true in certain areas, I say to these people with lenses, change your perspective. Human capital is one of our strongest assets because independent thought, creativity and conscious, which are what produces unique and innovative ideas, cannot be computer programmed.

With multinational companies and international institutions, many also believe that our world revolves around them. We need these companies to function and they are too big to fail, because the ripple effect will be devastating. They served a purpose where the money acquired by these entities trickles down to small businesses like your local barbershop.".

There was no need to state the obvious, that they were wrong. The group of friends knows from their daily lives that the reasoning is flawed.

"To support people, we have to create an economy that is set to serve the people. Meet them where they are, no matter where they are and who they are. Not controlled by any country or institution.

The perfect medium for this economy is the internet. It connects the world and has no boundaries. No borders and no walls. According to financial technology experts, in the future, technology will be more valuable than the company that created it, more powerful than any institution or country. That is what Bitcoin is and what it will do and bring to the people."

Brad is laughing.

"Brad, what is wrong with you? Why are you laughing?" Moto asks.

Brad continues to laugh and responds, "It just all clicked in my head and I pictured a Bitcoin flying through the air from computer to computer with a red cap and it shows up at your front door. As soon as you open the door, the sound effects - dun dun du duna - queued with his red cape flying and the wind flying only on him in that superhero stance. You know what I'm talking about."

"Nooooooooo." Lars cracks up.

"No. No. No, you don't. You know you're wrong. You're disrespectful," Sam adds.

"I'm serious though, this can work!" exclaims Moto. He is ecstatic.

"After all that, Moto, and that is the big name reveal?" inquires Brad.

Moto makes a face, and Sam, Lars, and Brad laugh even more.

"If I can continue before I was rudely interrupted," Moto states sarcastically.

"It is interesting," Joe states. "Human capital is power. Part of the reason why China's economic reforms capitalism are changing the world market, the reason why many European countries provide free college education to their citizens."

"Exactly, think about it. The perks and the conveniences of being able to send money to your friends around the world with ease without having to explain why and without people questioning your reasons and without the costly fees and collection of your personal information. It's the ultimate anonymity network to protect our privacy and our transactions for every day regular people, like you and me..."

Sam interjects, "You are far from the average person, Moto."

"It sounds good, but there are of course some things to think through," Lars mumbles.

Sam thinks to himself; this is an opportunity. Bitcoin. It could be digital gold; Moto is on to something.

He can come up with a better name than that. Sam can hear people saying now, what is a Bitcoin? What kind of name is that? Is it just literally a gold coin? Sam guesses it was a play on the Gold Rush, such a cliché.

Everyone declines to get involved in Moto's ponzi scheme. Sam had a family to think about and couldn't take the risk. He can lose a lot with the wrong investment, including his own business. The friends said their goodbyes, promised to keep in touch, and left Sam's home for the night.

Sam ponders over Moto's idea for a few weeks. Sam is not completely sold on the idea but was curious. The operation of this type of platform requires significant electricity and computing power, at least at the beginning. Access is achieved first through the investment in the technology and advancements made, over time the costs of computing power and electricity will decrease, to enable even greater use and access. This is important because these costs are on the user. But it would be an investment in energy efficient tools, and high-quality computers and hardware with ability to solve mathematical equations quickly. How can users be convinced to make such a long-term investment and how could we drive people to engage in beyond the technology savvy and the computer programmer person? In exchange for the user's electricity, they receive a few Bitcoins as a reward.

Sam cannot pinpoint exactly where the nickname Moto comes from. It must have been when Moto took the police motorcycle for a joyride straight through, what was the front door of Ford Hall. They were really rebelling against capitalism back then. They camped out for weeks, living in tents in front of National Bank in protest to the economic depression precipitated by Fortune 500 companies and the usual culprit, Wall Street, and their best friend—the real estate mortgage tycoons overvaluing the market and their assets, stealing money from everybody and then having the nerve to declare bankruptcy and pay their CEOs millions to resign and retire.

So many people lost everything, including Moto's family. Sam was okay but Moto had nothing. He built himself back up. Moto became a computer programmer. Not many were so lucky. Moto always had the inquisitive mind and tech skills to get ahead. But it seemed Moto was so gun-holed on breaking all strings with the institutions that betrayed the trust of the public and Uncle Sam. The government allowed the institutions to get away with everything and bailed them out. They said the banks and corporations were too big fail. It was evident that Moto did not think so. And it was clear that Moto is moving forward with his Bitcoin invention.

Perhaps it's just the nature of the risk, better yet, the excitement about a new technological innovation. He is still figuring out how to convince people that the investment is worth their time, to be a part of something great, greater than themselves, and to have a sense and need for belonging. The longing to challenge rules and the society structure, this could be potential drivers for users. Sam had to sit down with Moto and brainstorm some ideas.

Sam picked up the phone and dialed Moto. Dial tone. Silence. Dial tone. Moto picked up right before the third ring.

"Hello."

"Hey, Moto. How are you doing?" Sam begins.

"Good. What's going on?"

"Nothing in particular, I wanted to pick your brain more about this coin thing."

"Yeah, sure no problem, you should definitely come to my house so we can discuss," Moto states.

"I don't want to take up too much of your time. I just have a few questions, more so curious than anything."

"Don't be silly." Moto states. "Come over, I'm more persuasive in person. We will be free to talk, just me and you. Besides I do not believe you have even been to my house."

"I will swing by after work tomorrow. Let's say around 6:30," Sam responds.

"Yeah, that works."

"Okay. See you then."

"You know I am glad you called." states Moto.

"Sure. Later."

After Sam got off work the next day, he headed straight for Moto's house. He got there around 7:00 p.m. and since he got to Moto's he could not take his eyes off this painting hanging from the living room wall.

It was provocative. The naked body surrounded by an air of darkness. She looked alone, longing for a connection. That connection appeared to manifest in the form of chains,

chains that linked her to a mirror. The reflection staring back at me through the mirror was a body of numbers.

Moto interrupts Sam's thoughts, "Don't think too hard or narrow."

"The painting is jarring," Sam replies.

"That is why I bought it. It's always about perspective. How we view the world depends on the perspective." Moto pours a drink.

"Is this what is behind this Bitcoin thing?"

"I mean, this is about using technology to create financial independence, instead of people dependent upon institutions to verify their own money and get permission when, where and how they use it." Moto replies.

Sam takes on Moto's argument. "We work and live in a bureaucratic capitalist society. Profits have always been put before everything. This is the free market."

Moto jolts up from the sofa and clanks his glass on the table. "Let's be honest. This is more than about profit, this is about power! Big business controls the economy and the restraints placed on those fighting to create opportunity."

"Yes, so big business pulls the strings. This cannot be stopped. You are fooling yourself if you think you can or Bitcoin can," Sam offers.

"Remember perspective. This is not about stopping big business per se, but about changing the business model so that profits are not made at the expense of people," Moto states.

"That sounds nice, but there will always be those at the top and people at the bottom." Sam takes a drink.

"We can flip that on its head, Sam."

"How, no government, no bank involvement," Moto stated matter of fact.

Sam states. "You sound like you've been reading too many conspiracy blogs. How are people going to make money with no government involvement, when the government prints the money?"

"Not if the economy is purely electronic." Moto replies.

"That has already been done where transactions are facilitated on the internet. It is a booming sector for all businesses," Sam states.

Moto responds, "No. The money is purely electronic, not based on the US dollar or any other paper money."

"Moto, money that you can only use on the internet does not seem lucrative to anyone. There is no value to it, so why would people use it?"

"More and more of our transactions everyday occur over the internet," Moto says. "Tangible money is becoming obsolete. The value of currency is mathematically based anyway, we don't need to physically touch money to make its value or know its value."

"You want to create another DarkNet, but for the working class?" Sam asks.

"No. We are not hiding or engaging in any type of criminal behavior. This will be public on the World Wide Web," Moto answers.

"A public network that is anonymous. For what, what is the point? I need some more Jack." Sam holds out his glass.

Moto tips the bottle and liquor flows on top of the ice. "Enabling the free movement of money, mathematical computations and unique hash numbers could be automatically generated to identify transactions in minutes. People can earn money by investing their time and energy into the infrastructure. This is done by the miner lending their electrical power to verify the transaction history and its validity in the chain. The people will literally power the economy. See my friend, this is the last return of the hippy, the Rebel against capitalism!"

"But don't you still run up against the same issue that only the people with enough access and money can afford to power the platform? It would take high speed internet connection, quality computers with extensive computing power capacity and high electricity bills."

"We have work to do to figure out how more people can access and benefit, but the economy model is solid. No banks, no government, no institutions," Moto states.

Sam thinks all in all, it is a good idea. Yes, it could be digital gold. It most definitely can. "Where do we get started Moto and how do we build the foundation of the block-chain?"

"That is what we have to figure out. I need your skills and ideas. We need top computer programmers, coders, and hackers. That is what I have you and Sean for," chuckles Moto.

"To take over the world?" He asks.

The obstacles and risks were more than apparent, but the vision seems to have already captured Sam's mind. There is a chance this can work.

CHAPTER 2

CATCHING FLIGHTS

———

Sitting in the seat, tapping his feet, Sean is fuming inside.

I can't believe this! This makes absolutely no god-damn sense!

But here I am sitting at JFK airport, waiting on the red eye flight to London. I could kill my boss and his incompetent son, who still manages to be Chief Financial Officer after this royal fuck up.

I told him last week that the company needed him to transfer two million dollars to the company overseas checking account, so that our subsidiary can have access to it. This was supposed to be done by Friday, or it would not arrive by the time the subsidiary needed the money, which is Wednesday. Today is fucking Tuesday and guess who didn't send the transfer. Yup good old, Ron!

So now I have to clean up the mess.

I still must deal with the headache of submitting paperwork to TSA and IRS. But the hassle is outweighed by the $30,000 saved. This is just what happens when your boss hires his son to run the financial arm of a multi-billion-dollar company because it's his birthright. I am supposed to be at my friend's house hanging with Moto and the gang. I have not seen them in forever and I know they are talking shit right now about me.

My inner thoughts are interrupted by barking.

"Sean, we need you to come with us." A white male in his mid-thirties, strapped with a gun on his right side, and his hand on top of the gun holster motions to me with his left hand.

He did not see the DHS officers approaching him, fitted in military gear.

"For what?"

"Sir, we need to ask you a couple questions about the large sum of money you are trying to leave the United States with?"

He stammers, "I... I... uhh... I submitted all the paperwork from my company to you and completed the declaration form."

"Sir, that is precisely why we are here. We saw your declaration form and need to ask you some questions."

"Am I under arrest?"

"No, but we would like for you to come with us, this is a matter of national security."

"I am a U.S. citizen and I have authorization by my company as the Senior Financial adviser to take this money with me to give to our subsidiary company in London. Here is my company card with my name on it. I can also give you the CEO contact information and you can call him and ask him."

"Sir, just come with us."

He did not realize how long and slow the walk from the airline gates were from the security terminal. But he was eerily reminded as people stare at him walking with DHS officers surrounding him. He was not handcuffed but he did not need to be. The formation of the DHS officers told the airport onlookers all they need: he is a security threat. And while the officers did not tell him he is under arrest, he knew he could not leave freely to go anywhere nor board his flight.

He is put into a cold dark room, nothing but a metal table and bench. It feels like an hour before anyone came in to speak to me.

Thump. Folders and papers fall out of a box slammed on the metal table.

"What time is it?" he asks.

"10:00 p.m., but I do not think that is what you should be focusing on," the officer replies.

"My flight leaves at 11:20 p.m. and I have less than an hour to be at the gate for boarding."

"Sir, I just have a few questions. If you answer them honestly, then you will be on your way. If not, missing your flight will be the least of your worries."

"Okay, what do you want to know?"

"Where did you get the $2,000,000?" the officer asks.

"From my company, we are in the financial asset management business. I told the other officer that before and put it on the declaration form."

"I am asking you the questions now. Where did the money specifically come from?"

"Same answer. We manage the financial assets of major Fortune 500 corporations, and we withdrew the money from our bank, so that we can get the money to our subsidiary in London. The CFO missed the bank transfer deadline, and so it is cheaper for us to bring the money directly to our partners and colleagues in London than to wire the funds."

"Why did you not just have your bank transfer the money then?", the officer asks.

Sean exasperated, states, "To complete a wire of that amount of money takes normally two to three business days with multiple transaction fees charged by the bank. I understand that this is just the cost of doing business, but an overnight wire has a hefty transaction cost—the convenience, expediency, currency conversion fees, and the low exchange rate."

Internally Sean was fuming. This whole process was testing his patience. In the end, he would be robbed. The foreign bank wants their piece of the pie too. You may send $100,000 but the recipient only actually receives maybe $95,000, whereas, under pure currency conversion with actual currency exchange rate, it would be closer to $98,000. It's ridiculous.

In the case of $2 million, that is a loss of about $30K.

So now Sean is here stuck at the airport, subject to interrogation because today this is still the cheapest way to send money quickly by booking a round-trip flight last minute and physically bringing the money to London. Fucking ridiculous right! Video streams come from the space station, but money cannot be moved from point A to point B without costing more money.

"What are they using the money for, Sean?" the officer asks.

"As a subsidiary they are also in the financial asset management business and will use the money for an upcoming project, covering the costs of overhead, supplies, and the new tool resource development," Sean tells the officer.

"How do you know that this is how they are going to use the money?"

"Ahh...because that is what they told us and explained in their project proposal request, and we have a contract with them, requiring them to use the money as directed in the contract." Sean states.

"But how are you going to really know, if you are in the United States and they are over there in London?" the officer asks.

"I do not know if you are aware, but this is the way business is conducted. We are an international company, a multi-billion-dollar company. Like I told the other officer, you can call the CEO. His number is 949-65---"

The officer cuts him off and proceeds. "I do not need to speak with him, I am speaking with you. Is the money going to be used to pay bribes?"

Brad answers, "What? No way!"

"Are you sure? This is a significantly large sum of money."

"Did you not just hear me, Officer? Like I said, we are a multi-billion-dollar company, you can look us up."

"Did your company file complete taxes for all your company earnings last year?"

"Yes."

"Where are you incorporated?"

"Delaware."

"Is this supposed subsidiary in London just a shell company to hide your money for tax evasion and obscure transactions to engage in illegal activity?"

Sean unequivocally shakes his head. "Definitely not. Absolutely not. We are very profitable and make a lot of money for a lot of clients advising on investments, asset sales, and transactions. And we pay all our taxes. Maybe if I can just get our CEO on the phone, he can explain everything and clear up any issues."

"You know lying to a federal officer is a crime, so is corruption, fraud and material support for terrorism."

"Terrorism!? Wait a minute!" Sean lifts his hands up. "Hold on now. None of that is going on. I don't know where you are getting your information from, but there must be a mistake. Interrogating me for nothing, matter of fact I want a lawyer, I am not saying nothing else until I my lawyer gets here. You can direct all questions to my lawyer!"

"This is a matter of national security. You have no rights, NONE!"

"I want a lawyer!" Brad demands.

The officer responds, "Well good luck with that. You will be waiting a long time. We are going to see if anything changes after you been here for a few hours," grimaced the Officer as he shoved his papers and notepad into a folder and headed to the door.

"Officer! I need to use the bathroom."

"I need to know everything about where this money came from and where it is going and then I can help you. You help me, I help you. Are you going to help me with that?"

"I told you what I know and will only answer any further questions with my attorney present."

The officer nods his head in acknowledgment while he turns the knob on the door. He partly exits the door when he turns around to face Sean, using his body to go in between to hold the door open. He smiles then leaves.

* * *

In London, Henderson Financial's subsidiary was melting down under the pressure. Employees were stacking their resignation letters on the asset manager's desk.

Ron made promises to George that the London office will receive a huge infusion of cash, but they did not receive it. With their impending contract financial obligations, the London office made some tough decisions. The loans are supposed to delay liability, but the people lost. The London subsidiary could not afford to pay their staff and fulfill their contractual obligations. Right under their nose, there had been skimming off the top. Relativity small portions of financial assets there were paid to manage, somehow were diverted to third party offshore accounts. One percent here and two percent there did not raise flags initially. But when those percentages were added up over time, and management could not account for the discrepancies, someone would have to take the blame. This was not about responsibility but about saving face and salvaging the little remaining respect and trust of their clients.

The executives in the United States have lost all confidence in the London management, which is why they had added all these conditions on the requested project related funding and data intensive reports, delaying the transfer of the funds in the first place. We had not been entirely transparent with them about the state of the London subsidiary, but they only knew what they needed to know. Once we received the cash, there would be no more problems. We would hire everyone back. There was no need to worry them in the United States when it wouldn't matter in 48 hours. George thought he had it all under control.

Knock on the door.

"Sir, Ron from U.S. headquarters is on the line."

"Okay, patch him through." George responds.

"Good afternoon Ron, well good morning to you guys in the States."

"I just wanted to update you and the team in London, that the funds may be slightly delayed." George mouths the word "shit," and mutes his line. Ron continues speaking but George is not hearing him.

Ron tells George, "Sean will bring the cash in person to the London office but will be delayed due to some issues at the airport. Remember we will need to see the books and records, and likely want to sit down with management and supervisors at the London office to discuss priorities, next quarter growth prospectus, and risk assessments. Okay?"

George unmutes the phone. "Yes, that works." He then takes the phone off speaker.

"Hey Ron, do you have a couple more minutes to spare? I just want to run some things by you."

"Yes, go ahead."

"The office in London is barely above water. This may or may not be something the head office in the States is aware of, but it has come to my attention that we were hacked. Our finance system, it is not something that we noticed because it was small, insignificant amounts taken at a time. But with Sean coming here, I think it might be best to have him set up new credit and bank accounts for the London office here, since he has the power to give authorization."

"Why are we just hearing about this?" Ron asks.

George responds, "We have it under control. It is not like this is the first time we have dealt with a hack. It is commonplace now in this industry and we have insurance that covers most of the money that was stolen."

"George, I need to bring this to my father and the board. I imagine that there are security measures that will need to be taken."

"Wait a minute. I told you this because I wanted advice. I thought you would understand my need to address this myself I oversee London. This is my responsibility the head office put me in this position for a reason. You know how it feels to just be a puppet you don't need to tell your father. We must come to him with a solution not just a problem. If no solution, that will likely mean my termination."

"I understand, George, but they have to know. This could compromise our entire internal network and we have no idea how much damage has been done with the delay in sharing this information with us. This can also be a PR nightmare if our clients find out, which may be inevitable for liability, we must provide notice sooner rather than later. Perhaps controlling the narrative can shape this as an isolated incident."

"Ron, I assure you, we have a reputable independent expert team on this. That is part of the security line of funding requested for the project."

"You're trying to hide behind this request and substitute this for the actual disclosure required?" Ron asks.

George answers, "Come on. I know for a fact that you do not do everything by the book, but as long as it gets done then it does."

"How much time do you need?" Ron asks.

"Forty-eight hours at the max," George replies.

"Okay. Forty-eight is what you get. What is the fiscal status of the London office now? Tell me, because Sean is going to be able to see right through any books and record keeping manipulation. Anything that seems off will make him suspicious."

"Well we had to let most of the employees go on a temporary basis until we get the influx of cash from the project funding."

"No one is working!?" Ron asks.

George responds, "Supervisors and higher management staff are still here."

"So that is what, maybe fifteen people. But over 100-person support personnel staff and contract consultants' desks will be empty. That won't raise suspicions at all," Ron breathes into the phone.

Ron continues. "You have to bring them back. Perhaps our clients may be interested in investing in a new product, exclusive to clients with Henderson Financial. They can get in on the ground floor before it even hits the market and reap all the rewards. I mean we are looking out for their best interests. The commission from these investments can go to cover the costs of overhead for a while."

"Really, that could work. What is the product, why didn't the head office tell me about this?" George asks.

"This is not from the head office. I just heard about this from the London office. What is the name again? It's on the tip of my tongue, you just told me George, but it slips my mind."

George responds, "I do not follow. You just told me about the product."

"Remember George, there is a new product that your clients in London can invest in. Only you know the name of this product and what it entails. Only you," Ron responds suggestively. He continues, "Be smart, make sure transactions are accurate, nothing more, nothing less. You know sometimes investments don't make positive returns, it's a risk they knowingly take, and we cannot be responsible for the consequences of these risks, anything else George? I have to prepare for some meetings today."

"Got it! Are you going to your father, Ron?" George sighs.

"George did you hear me before? I am trying to help you because you know we Upsilon brothers, but you got to help yourself too. You got the weekend to make it right. I got to go."

The hours seem to go so fast, as George picks up the phone trying to convince one client to invest in the exclusive product Lotus pre-market launch, and then dials another client. George is scrolling through his client database and punching the numbers on his office phone, one after the other in a somewhat robotic fashion. The voice on the other side of the phone was George's only company tonight. He wonders whether the desperation is coming out in his voice as he makes the pitch. The moon is peaking out of the blue sky. He did not eat dinner because there is no time to eat. He doesn't even physically put the phone down on the receiver after each call. He just hits the receiver to get a new dial tone to begin a new call. The phone handle practically glued to his hand and ear.

The hours are speeding by in London. But in the United States, the hours are going so slow for Sean. The DHS officers would not let up on him, while they ripped through the money looking for counterfeits. They would probably also let the dogs get a smell of it too for any drug residue. They were ripping through his background too.

Social media and public information could reveal a lot about a person, but it also hid a lot of the complexities of a person because a lot of the public information is not the individual per se, but a version of the individual. Social media creates and develops a public persona, identifies the public persona, but not the actual person, just the person that was public, nothing more. However, this public persona classifies and profiles Sean forever. He did not care either way. A part of him feels like he did not have anything to hide. Yes, maybe he works for a somewhat unethical company, but it is a job. Henderson Financial often toed the line and did everything even unethical things right up to crossing over to unlawful. But being unethical is not a crime. But the idea that strangers with ulterior agendas could use his public persona to prejudge him and decide whether he was a criminal or not somewhat disturbed him.

It felt like half a day passed by the time the officer came back into the room with a cup of coffee. He looks different than yesterday. No more facial hair and fresh clothes.

"How was your night?" The officer smiles at him.

"Did you get in touch with my lawyer?"

"I believe he is on his way," he responds.

"Good." Sean states. "Officer, may I use the restroom?"

"Not right now. But I did bring you some coffee. I heard it curbs hunger. You must be hungry. The sooner we can get you to cooperate, the sooner we can get you out of here and you can hit the brick oven pizza place. They don't open until noon, but I think we will be enjoying each other's company well past noon anyway. Am I right?"

Sean huffs, fidgets in the metal chair, leans back, folds his arms across his chest. He stretches his arms up and looks up to the fluorescent lights.

The door to the interrogation room opens wide, the doorknob slams against the wall, as his attorney storms through.

She looks him straight in the eye. "My client is leaving now! Anything he said without me present is inadmissible! This is harassment and abuse of authority. Every single dollar of Henderson Financial money better be accounted for and in my client's possession when he leaves here, or we are going to have another problem!"

"Take it up with Congress and the Executive Lady. I'm just doing my job."

Sean's attorney continues to stare down the officer, "Let's go Sean."

Sean and his attorney leave. He heads straight to the airline customer service to re-book him on the next flight. Re-booking goes smoothly. His attorney hands him a coffee and bag. Sean opens the bag and immediately eats the bagel. He is starving. He is exhausted and he needs a shower and clean clothes.

His attorney begins talking. "What happened to you is unacceptable. We are going to find every procedure and any protocol that the officers did not abide by, and make sure they are fired. Now I need to know, what did you say to them?"

"I didn't say anything. I was mostly trying to get information out of them. And I asked for a lawyer."

"Okay good. Any questions they asked you that caught your attention? Like something I should be aware of?"

"I don't think so. I mean it's ridiculous, I missed my flight. They had no basis; all the paperwork was completed. You know me I don't cut corners. This whole mess is on the CEO, Ron. I got to get to London. Thanks for coming down and handling this for me."

"Okay. I will follow-up."

Sean heads straight to the airline VIP lounge. He relaxes in bed pod, drinks and food on the coffee table, as he waits on his flight.

Boarding begins on his flight and he boards the plane. In first class, there is another drink waiting for Sean. After a couple sips, he is sleeping until his plane lands in London. At luggage pickup he calls the CEO, confirming his arrival in London. Exiting the airport, he gets into a taxi to the hotel. Upon check-in, he struggles to make it to his room, where he collapses on the bed.

The next morning, it is cloudy in London. Sean visits some of the sites in route to deposit the cash for their subsidiary in the bank.

When he finally gets to George's office, he is ready to get out of there. He wants to continue to explore the city of London and doesn't want work to take over the rest of the day. If the paperwork is all together for him to review the records and bookkeeping, Sean can quickly review everything and be on his way.

This doesn't happen. When he gets there, nothing is ready. George puts Sean in the conference room. Every so often a person would come into the conference room, placing a file box, or stack of papers, never the same person. Most of the records are electronic, but with Sean conducting a semi-audit, he needs to see the documents that support the records that were the basis for the record and book-keeping.

Sean gets to work. He pours over the record keeping book, line by line of each document. He notices gaps in information, things didn't make sense. Maybe there were documents in the file cabinet room. He goes sifting through the cabinets. He notices slips, handwritten invoices. Sean goes through the file cabinet room, drawers open and close. He pulls documents and spreads them out all on the floor. Sticky notes are everywhere, signaling follow-up or questionable transaction. Sean gets up from the file cabinet room drawer floor. Sean gathers the documents and heads back to the conference room to organize the documents again. What he sees shocks him. He gets up, swings the conference door and his head pops out to the hallway to yell "George, I need to see you in here now!" Sean commands. "George, what is this line item, 'inside consultant' for $10,000 for?"

"We had to use a contractor to perform some assessments for the project funding, but could not, well did not want to, hire someone as an employee, as that would require full time benefits, health care etc, and negotiation rights. We needed the job done right away with as few complications as possible." George responded as detailed as he could.

Sean lifts off sticky notes from another document, "And here there is another for 'inside consultant' same amount, it was made yesterday."

"Wait, that shouldn't even be in the files for review." George states.

"What do mean?" Sean asks George.

"Well it was yesterday, generally paperwork is not processed that quickly, and not subject to this review now."

Sean questions him further, "I have it right here. Is it coming out of project financing or not? What is it for?"

"Uhh. The office here, we had to pay for policy advocacy to the Parliament."

"For a tax bill or something?"

"Yea, I believe so," says George.

"That is interesting because we have funding set aside in a separate account for legislative expenses, George. Why didn't you just request money from there? I don't remember hearing about any impending legislation here."

George replies. "Yea, it's kind of under wraps. It's being talked about, not actually introduced yet. But I got information from good sources, so we can get ahead of this thing."

"Okay. This new project seems to also heavily rely upon outside consultants and contractors. Should we just be hiring people full time, I mean looking at the spew of talent that we can have at our disposal, versus paying various third parties more in the future?" Sean flipped through papers.

"I mean, that is ultimately a decision for you guys in the main office in California," George states uneasily.

Sean's phone rings. He walks around the desk to the coat rack to get the phone out of his blazer. Speaking into the phone he says, "Sean Jefferson. Yes, that was me. I'm with Harper & Doyle." Sean pauses.

"Yes, Henderson Financial is under us." Sean pauses again. Indiscernible noise is coming through the phone. Sean looks over at George. "Oh, I see." Sean pauses. "Come again?" He does not speak again, intently listening to the person on the other end. "Let me get a pen, to get this down."

Sean snaps at George, makes a writing hand gesture. George grabs him a pen and notepad.

"Can you repeat that?" Sean asks into the phone.

George is watching Sean jot down December 2007 - present. "How much again? No that must be wrong, some kind of mistake. Can we have you look into that and investigate that?" Sean pauses. "Yes, I can come back in. I got to make a few calls, but I should be there in less than an hour. And put a hold on that deposit from today." Sean takes a breath. "You can't! Why not?!" Sean listening. "I don't want to hear about bank procedures on cash deposits, transaction holds, or next business day rules. I was just there this morning, a few hours ago, it could not have been processed that quickly?!" He pauses again. "I know it was in cash. You said that already. No, I don't want to be put on hold. I need to speak with your manager. Well a supervisor then, whomever you report to. Matter of fact, the bank CEO." ...

"I do not care where he is you better find him and make him available. And I am not leaving no damn message or sending an email. I am coming down to the bank and he better be there. Or we will be going to another bank and every penny including our U.S. accounts will be closed, going directly to your competitor, opening new accounts, and they will handle our billion-dollar portfolio!"

Sean hangs up the phone, throws it on the table and looks at George.

"Everything okay?" George asks Sean.

"Two million five hundred thousand, George!"

George clears his throat. It's dry. He pours a glass of water. Licks his lips and swallows.

"That was just the bank here in London. Does two million five hundred thousand mean anything?" Sean asks.

No answer from George.

"You signed off on this!? And for what? Where is the money going? Is that what those $10,000 line items were paying for? The Monthly payments due are $10,000 too?"

"I'm reporting this to the U.S. office." Sean puts his phone on speaker phone." It's dialing.

From the speaker, "Thank you for calling Harper & Doyle. How may I direct your call?"

"Hey Tina, this is Sean Jefferson."

"Hello Mr. Jefferson," the receptionist answers.

"Hello. Please connect me with Mr. Harper. It's urgent, involving the London office."

"Yes, of course. Hold on please."

"Don't be naive." George interjects. "This is how it works here. How do you think we get things done here in London? Everyone has to get paid; nothing is free." Sean cuts his eyes at George. "That is not the way we do business. You put our entire company in jeopardy!"

Music continues to play on the phone.

"You guys knew," George said sheepishly.

Sean responds, "Knew what? I didn't know anything!"

George responds, "I didn't say you, but California knows. We are not immune to the business practices of London. Everybody does. If I say no or refuse, we lose clients, mystery our credit lines are cut, and we no longer qualify for certain contract bids. Remember that article saying the London office was the last place that Chinese diplomat entered before disappearing? How do you think it went away? Better yet, why do you think the article came out in the first place?"

Mr. Harper's voice comes through, "Mr. Jefferson. How's everything at the London Office?"

"I'm here with George, who heads the London Office."

George speaks, "Hello Mr. Harper."

Sean resumes, "There are some discrepancies over here. Unaccounted for investments and missing funds among other discrepancies."

"How much? And to what extent?" asks Mr. Harper.

"The bank told me, the London office, we, are in the hole one million five hundred thousand. It's been going on since at last December 2007. I don't know exactly who here in London or even in California knew. But the head of the office here, George was involved. He is here with me now. There are suggestions of potentially extensive corruption. I recommend we tell legal, maybe get an outside firm to..."

Mr. Harper interrupts him, "You will do no such thing. We will handle this internally. What about the two million deposit?"

Sean exhales. "I'm trying to put a freeze on it. But the bank is talking about they already processed it and being credited toward the debt owed. They said they may be able to offer an additional line of credit, not at two million, but something if we need it, and will just have to complete the paperwork on that."

"That is unacceptable!" Mr. Harper states through the phone.

"I'm going down to the bank now. I'm taking George with me."

"No. You go down to the bank. George?! George?!"

"Yes." George states to Mr. Harper.

"You are fired! Clean out your desk and office. Leave the keys, company car, and credit card with Sean."

"What!" screams George.

"Call security if you have to Sean."

"Okay." Sean responds. "I'll call you when I'm at the bank." Sean is still on the phone with Mr. Harper.

"I cannot believe this! You knew! You told me to do it!" exclaims George.

"No!" Mr. Harper is stern. "You stole from this company! I built this company from the ground up with my own hands, and I am not going to let someone like you, take it from me! You are fired! And I mean it. If you do not go, you will not like what happens."

"Are you threatening me?!"

"This is on you too, Sean." Mr. Harper states.

"What?! How am I being held responsible for a division I do not have control over. That is your son who is supposed to be running the finances, not me! He is the CEO. If he allowed this to happen, which it is pretty clear to me that he did, then the only person to blame is yourself for putting an unqualified person in that position because he's your son."

Mr. Harper yells, "You lost two million dollars of my money!"

Sean responds, "No I'm working on it. We are going to get it back and hold George accountable for this bank loan and the actual stealing of your money!"

Mr. Harper talks over Sean. "If you cannot have self-accountability, we cannot have you on our team. I'll accept your resignation. See to it that I have a signed copy on my desk or sent to my email. Effective two weeks from today."

Sean is staring at the post it notes crowding the calendar on the wall.

"Did you just fire me over the phone?" he says into the phone.

Mr. Harper answers, "I suggested you resign. You are no longer meeting the quality and standards, we demand."

"I'm not meeting standards? What standards?" asks Sean.

The call ends.

CHAPTER 3

FOR THE PEOPLE

———

Moto wants to make his own money, computer programmer money. Something that people cannot touch, cannot really see, just a bunch of numbers and letters—computer code.

Sam poses, "How will people know it is real? Why will they believe it's not a scam?"

"This is what is done in tangible currency. Think about it." Moto responds.

"Well, the USD value is based on the economy fluctuations, which is based on supply and demand in the marketplace." Sam states.

Moto speaks, "Exactly. But forget the technical jargon, it's all Math. We do not have to physically touch supply and demand, but we know it exists."

Moto goes into his back pocket and pulls out rolling paper, a lighter, crumbled up cash, and a loose key. A pocketknife falls from Moto's lap to the mat. He rummages through the things in his pockets and straightens out a $20 bill that he displays and continues, "The paper the USD is printed on is not the basis of the USD value. Market behavior is, this is Math."

Math is the foundation for coding. As an internet-based invention, it's just numbers sequenced to execute functions and actions. The Bitcoin can be the emergence of a new economy model. The most important part of the company is the people. Yes, the people, your neighbor, the school coach, your dentist, and even the mailman that will power the platform.

"So how will this work in practical terms, Moto? We need to lay this out. I need paper and a pen."

"Let's start with identifying what we want. For one thing, we want it to be secure from hackers and third-party actors," says Sam.

"We also want anonymity. Add it to the list Sam.

"Strong but quick verification of ownership and transactions."

"Decentralized system too," says Moto.

Sam spells out independence on the paper.

Moto sets up his Think Pad and scurries to the kitchen for snacks. Cabinets and freezer open, and ice drops into glasses.

"The pizza should be here soon." Sam informs Moto.

"Okay, you got your laptop and battery pack?" Moto asks Sam.

Sam responds, "Yup, right here. Let's get to work."

Moto crashes on the floor in the living room. Caffeinated sodas and energy drinks surround him. Sam flops on the bean bag chair.

Everything is still in the room, Moto in his space and Sam is in his. Yet, the room is bustling, fingertips hitting keys, stroke after stroke, click after click. Once in a while, Sam steps out of his world of techno-beats and shouts something inaudible to Moto. Not really looking for a response, just needing an outlet to express, a quick break to get creative juices flowing when he got stuck.

Moto's eyes glaze over the desktop bar and notice the date, 06/19/2008. They had been up all night. The dark blinds mask the hours that had passed and the daylight. He stretches and pulls the earbuds out of his ears. Walking to the kitchen, he feels the cold tile floor. He grabs a soda out of the fridge. He crashes back in front of the screen and zones back out.

Keystrokes resume for hours.

Sam cuts across the living room, stepping over Moto to get to the bathroom. He takes a leak and cuts off the faucet before hitting the lights. Cutting across the living room again, he grabs a slice.

Once again, Sam immerses in the letters and numbers jumping across his screen.

Time keeps churning and the clock jumps ahead.

"Check out what I have coded," Moto shouts as he pulls the headphones out of Sam's right ear. "This is just preliminary and not fully executed." Moto gets up and follows him. "So, likely still bugs that we will have to work through. Especially since I have been shot up on carbonated caffeine for what, thirty or so hours," Sam yawns and stretches, "I know I get that it's rough. You need some better furniture."

"Just check it out. I'm executing the code now to test it."

Keystrokes, Moto hits the enter key. More keystrokes. Enter.

"You see that a digital record is created for this transaction. There is also here embedded in the code, essentially a footprint verification of prior transactions from origination. Now I make another transaction with part of my value of the last transaction." Moto clicks. "Not only is the ownership of this transaction verified, but also my prior transaction and original ownership. And it will continue to build on each other."

"No single transaction can be severed from its historical verification process?" asks Sam.

"Theoretically," Moto answers. "The value of the block chain, that's what I call it. Is in the digital footprints that verify ownership and security. Public and private keys are assigned to each user on the platform. Only persons with a public and private key can access the platform to engage in a transaction. With every transaction, a footprint is recorded upon use of a public key, assigned to a user. While both the private and public key is required to engage in a transaction, only the public key is visible to the public to verify the ownership of the store of value being used in each transaction. As more transactions are engaged with a particular public key, the data from those transactions are layered on top, built upon each other, to create a transaction history. The public key is visible, but still anonymous as the public key is made up of numbers that are generated by a cryptographic algorithm. There is personally identifying information of the actual person in the public key."

Sam states, "Okay, so to make sure I'm understanding correctly, the transaction history essentially verifies the ownership of each store of value to permit a current transaction by verifying each transaction of the store of value from origin to present. But how are the value or good exchanges in the transaction validity tested?"

"Well Sam, I am thinking that each store of value is assigned a unique identifier, like a serial number, so that it is traceable. So even where an individual Bitcoin used is used separate from the other Bitcoins part of the original transaction, the history of ownership and transaction history of each Bitcoin is recorded and able to be verified as well. Only upon verification of each store of value and transaction hash number, is the transfer of value for the current transaction verified and allowed to proceed," Moto states.

"This is good. I'm not quite finished with my coding, but this may be the point to begin to integrate the coding and work together. If this blockchain works, it will need to be integrated into the platform coding. We have been at this for a while. I feel like my body has become one with this bean bag." Sam shifts, emitting the sound of a salt and pepper shaker.

Moto gets up from the floor, "I think we went through all the pizza and beer, but I can pop some hot pockets in the microwave."

"If this works you will be able to buy a couple pizza franchise stores with Bitcoin," Sam touts.

"That is cool."

"That reminds me Moto. How will the payer pay and how will the payee retrieve their payment in a secure way so that both parties are able to stay anonymous and protected? That is what I have been focusing on."

"That is a must. I have not thought that far through at this point. Ideally we will want the payment to be secure so that only the payee is able to access the payment."

"It will need to be unique and have unique access. I'm thinking, coding a separate portal on the platform, where the payee in the transaction is provided limited access that is only accessible by a combination of the payee's unique public and private keys. The private key that is uniquely tied to the user would be required to retrieve the payment from the portal. Do we want to enable users to be able to send payment to their PayPal or something, since we are not using banks?" Sam poses the question to Moto.

"No, the setup is for this platform to be entirely independent."

"Hmmm," says Sam. "People are earning or buying currency to pay for transactions on a platform, but 'no' means to cash out?"

"Yes, for now at least," Moto continues, "we can set up entirely unique hash for that user for payments too. Okay. Okay. I can see how this can work."

Sam struggles to get up from the bean bag chair. "We will have to design the system to prevent hacks or at least make it more difficult to prevent breaches. Then a separate unique hash for each user's particular transaction must be generated automatically per transaction. That only the payer can access, not visible by the payer."

"This could be difficult. To program for an infinite number generated automatically, which by in large will pass the number of actual Bitcoins in the universe." Moto poses rhetorically. "But not impossible. If each user is assigned a unique immortal email address online, we can maintain the user's privacy. Just hear me out on this Sam, through this email as verified and tied to the public and private key, the platform automatically generates a link to retrieve payment from the transaction without any payment information being sent to the payee. You follow me?"

"Yeah, so as blockchain is creating a record to verify the transaction as through the public key, the completion of the transaction is acknowledged through a private key that is tied to the user's bitcoin email address. Only accessible on the platform, of which you must sign in with a username and password and verify private key. Only through the private key, can the user actually transfer Bitcoin from one account to another."

"No exceptions and no reset button for the private key." Moto takes the words right out of Sam's mouth, "We will need to develop the baseline mining code so that users are able to mine the Bitcoin to power the platform."

"How often should we update the code? We probably need a team dedicated to development." Sam states.

"The platform is public Sam, and so should the baseline code. We want this to be a tool that can be used by the people and be a means to access. The technology development should not be in the hands of a few selected persons either."

He thinks that with the code out in the public, computer programmers will take it from there. Adding and manipulating the code to make use easier, more efficient, and develop the platform. To attract beyond the technology savvy and computer programmer market to the general public, there will be a need to package the baseline mining code into software that users download onto their computer with instructions on how Bitcoin works, the concept and functioning of mining and the block chain.

This can be done at no cost to us but by open source software developers, motivated by innovation, seeking to create something new, different or better by improving on the baseline code.

"I think we kind of got it." Moto pops a couple of M&M peanuts from the bowl into his mouth and cleans his hands on his pant legs. He grabs the papers off the floor, as he tapes the organized papers with chip residue fingerprints from handling the papers, he presses his lips and nods his head in a sense of accomplishment. His eyes are bright with hope and twitching from no sleep but the light in his eyes keeps them open.

"We have more to do. But let me visualize this."

This execution of the blockchain is like nothing ever seen before, it is simple in concept though. In a snapshot, the blockchain is made up of blocks of data, chained together. With layers of unique hash numbers generated per transaction, that essentially serve as building blocks, with each transaction being built, layered on top of prior transactions in a snapshot, the public and private key framework will serve as a barrier to obtaining the true identity of the user. The only thing visible is the public key, nothing more.

Sam envisions that even to attempt to hack, which he believed would be impossible, would require at a minimum the hacking of thousands of transactions, finding the private key to thousands of users, finding the unique identification code to each individual coin involved in the current transaction, manipulating thousands of the ownership history and manufacturing thousands of historical transactions. By the time this is figured out, even if possible, another transaction takes its place, changing the transaction history and mandating further verification, and this process repeats itself, happening over and over. Not to mention that linking the private key to the unique user for the transaction would be virtually impossible because users are anonymous. The anonymity of the network significantly decreases security issues. Virtually not hack-able, it will take too much computing power.

Moto resumes talking, "Just like a hacker would need an immense amount of commuting power to hack transactions. We will need an immense amount of computing power to have transactions and transactional history verified accurately and quickly. I presume we are not going to provide the computing power to every single transaction forever. We will need the computing power of users of the platform but also persons not necessarily engaging in transactions."

"Why would random people not using the platform want to help the platform Moto, out of the goodness of their hearts?"

"No Sam, but we can provide an incentive. We can give them Bitcoin in exchange for their computing power to verify transactions. Both powering the platform and increasing use and knowledge about Bitcoin."

"You are building in platform users by design."

Moto begins to draw and write on loose scrap paper, creating a visual graph of the process. Pointing with a marker, Moto presents, "That is how the platform will work. We need everyone, first the technology savvy and computer programmers to develop software. Second, we need the people to use the network by engaging in transactions and purchases, —they will power the platform and of course we need the miners, who are part of the security, to establish proof of work through transaction verification and ownership."

No one is in control; everyone plays a role.

* * *

Sean is home now. Being fired over the phone was humiliating. He went to London to clean up the mistakes they made, but somehow, he was blamed. He had told his boys about it, they were not shocked, but Sean was. He stayed in London a few weeks after the call with Harper, he had to take care of some things. Those things had followed him back home to the United States. For the past couple days since getting home, he had been thinking about what to do next.

Well at first, he was anxious, calling colleagues from business school, seeing if they could get him in the door with one of their firms. He had the experience, academic credentials, and connections, but no calls back. He thought some of his old business school buddies were even actively blocking and dodging his calls.

Sean keeps his regular routine, up at 5:00 a.m. and out the door by 5:15 a.m. for his morning run. He is back by 5:45 a.m. to turn the coffee pot on, shower, and get dressed by 6:20 a.m. Sean finishes his coffee and he is out the door by

6:30 a.m. Usually he would head to the office to be ready to work by 7:00 a.m. but now he had nowhere to go. In the car, he decided to stop by one of the top firms in the business, where his business school buddy, Rick, works.

Rick's firm is not an exact competitor of his old firm. Sean did not care about any non-compete clause anyway. A lawsuit is the furthest thing on Henderson Financial's plate right now because they are dealing with a lot because of the London office. It is part of the reason why he is on the industry blacklist. No one is going to hire him. But it was worth it, he would have paid money to see the look on Mr. Harper's face when he got the call that the London office was raided. The competition is not going to hire him, anyway, so why not have some fun. He wanted to confront Mr. Harper in person, but he was prohibited from even entering the building by security. He settled for the next best thing, getting under his skin by getting cozy with the competition. Even if he cannot work for Rick's firm as an employee, maybe he can consult and advise.

"Good Morning. I am going up to see Rick Matthew with the Matthews Firm," Sean states to building security.

"Do you have an appointment sir?" the security officer asks.

"No. But Rick Matthews knows me. He should be expecting me." Sean replies.

"I'm sorry sir, appointments only."

"Let me just give him a call and he can sort this all out." Sean calls Rick. He is sent to voicemail, so he texts Rick, "Hey

I'm downstairs. I thought we could grab a coffee or breakfast. Just need a few minutes of your time, it's on me." Sean stares at his phone, watching to see when the text message is read and the three dot bubbles to appear, meaning Rick was typing a reply. Rick read the text message and replies, "What are you doing here?" Sean begins to type, "seriously" but deletes it. Sean texts him, "can you just come downstairs? It won't take long." Sean reads the text message, "Okay. Give me a sec."

"He is coming down." Sean states to security and walks off to the side to wait.

Endless numbers of people pass through the revolving doors. Everyone scans a key fob to go upstairs to their jobs in the glass office building. Floors 1–10 on the right and floors 11–20 on the left. Sean is looking in the direction of the left elevator. The Matthews firm name is on the outside of the building, one of the perks with having the largest spaces in an office building. Meaning paying the most money in an office space for a name, as your name on a building signaled prestige and power. In order to make money, you must spend money, and for most firms, Sean knows that means spending money to keep up appearances and expectations. Sean continues to wait for Rick.

The security officer noticing that Sean was still there for more than thirty minutes calls upstairs to the Matthews firm.

"Good morning. This is security downstairs, there is a man here waiting for Rick Matthews. He said he is a friend and that Mr. Matthews said he was coming down, but Mr.

Matthews did not come down, and the man is still here. Can you give Mr. Matthews this message? If he does not want this man here or wants us to let him upstairs, he can let us know. We cannot have people just standing in the building lobby, it's a security issue. I hope you understand."

Sean sees security looking at him. He pulls out his phone to check his text messages, nothing from Rick. He opens his email. He didn't expect to have any new emails but just wants to keep busy, look busy, and look important. He looks up from his phone to the security desk and security looks at him. A woman at the counter turns her head to look at what the security guard is looking at, him. Sean smiles at the woman. As he admires her, Rick walks into the lobby. Rick embraces the woman. While hugging her, he came in Sean's direct view. They're eyes connect and the woman hands Rick an envelope.

Rick did not expect for Sean to still be there. It was nearly 9:00 a.m. now. He walks over to Sean. "Hey man, let's talk outside." Rick and Sean push through the revolving doors to exit the building. Rick turns left. "So how is everything Sean?"

"Could be better, you know."

"You wanted to grab a coffee? Let's go to this latte spot." Rick states.

"I already had my coffee some time ago. You know, I was pushed out by Harper, made the fall guy. But you know I always come out on top."

"Of course," Rick replies.

"Do you know of any opportunities?" Sean asks.

"You know. When you first reached out, I talked to some people, put the word out. But you know with the current market, the men upstairs don't feel this is the time to make any significant changes."

"They don't feel?" Sean hands the cashier his card to pay for the lattes.

"You can't shake the tree too hard. You got to understand Sean."

"Enlighten me."

"Look, you know how this works. We are a small knit community and we have to look out for each other." Rick responds.

"You mean Harper and protecting the big ole boys."

Rick chuckles and turns to face Sean. "You can't seriously have thought that there would be no consequences after London. You made the wrong decision."

"So, I screw someone who screws me, and I'm to blame." states Sean.

"And you got screwed back," responds Rick.

"I'm blacklisted. This is the screwed back?"

"I wish I could help you," Rick answers Sean.

"Don't give me that. You didn't even have the guts to talk to me face to face. If it wasn't for that envelope, you wouldn't have even come downstairs, although you told me you were coming."

"You show up out of nowhere uninvited, no heads up or anything. And you expect me to jump for you?"

Sean stares at Rick and takes a deep breath. "We were friends. I thought you would have my back, at least some professional courtesy."

Rick pats Sean's shoulder. "It's not personal, it's business. It was great catching up with you, I got to head back though. Thanks for the coffee." Rick raises his cup. "Keep in touch." Rick gets up and walks away, turning left, in the opposite direction of his office. He didn't mean to really keep in touch, just pleasantries. Neither of them expected Sean to keep it, especially after today. The whole morning conversation was an exercise in pleasantries. Nothing was going to come from this conversation, and Sean knew. He barely took a sip of his latte and threw it out. Leaving the latte shop he texts Moto, "I'm on my way."

Sean got to Moto's house a little before 11:00 a.m. After college, Sean and Moto grew distant, with Sean going to work in corporate America. Moto was too principled. Sean felt judged as if he had betrayed Moto. But when it came down to it, they were different. But their pride prevented them from ever getting past their differences. At gatherings that their friends invited them to, they would briefly speak but just surface level. Moto was a little surprised when he saw Sean's text, and since Moto didn't respond, he didn't expect Sean to just show up, but Sean was in his living room, drinking. Sean is talking about his flight arrest and being fired.

"Bitcoin? Spoke with Brad for some legal help with the whole London situation. And you know he can't keep anything to himself. It's part of the reason why I wanted to stop by. Talk to you about this Bitcoin."

Moto smiles. "You can use the distraction or you want to get them back?"

"I think I'm still trying to figure that out. Of course, I want to come back on top, no question about that."

"You made my day, all of us will be doing this together," Moto states.

"I could use the fresh start. It doesn't seem like I will be working anywhere in corporate American anytime soon."

"Yeah, not going to happen but fuck them. Let's get started." Moto' puts his glass down. "Get you up to speed on what Sean and I have come up with." He walks away to his desk, there are stacks of paper on his desk with a bunch of other items. But tucked away in a draw is a binder that Moto pulls out.

"A binder?"

"How long have you been working on this?" Sean asked.

"Just a few months."

"A few months?"

"Yes, Sam and I began shortly after the game night."

"Okay. But how long have you been working on it? I know you Moto. You obsess over things, always got great ideas you just got to get them out into the world."

"Just open the binder. Give me your opinion."

Sean opens the binder. It's heavy. Different types of paper fill the binder. Notes mixed in with organized thoughts. Sean reads paragraphs. Then he would see a hand drawn diagram. Turning the page, bullet points and sporadic notes followed. There are pages tabbed. Seems like attempts at organization with notes to footnote here and there. Erasure marks and words crossed out with pen show that several attempts were made to draft and thoughts of different persons. There were even printouts of articles and other sources for their logic.

Moto is staring at him, patiently waiting. Hours now, Sean is going through the binder swiftly. Shifting every once in a while, but he was turning pages, and he was still there. That was a good sign if there was any.

"Moto, this Bitcoin can grab more than a share of the market. Have you done any research on if there is anything out there like this in the market?"

"Not really. Beyond just electronic transfers that use standard coding to verify bank to bank transfers, I think that is the closest if anything is close at all."

"I can do that for you if you want."

"You don't think there is enough there? You couldn't have read through it all?"

"I skimmed. But the most important piece that sums it all up is this diagram." Sean flips through the pages, he knew it was one of the tabbed pages (there were many tabbed pages). Flipping through the pages of the binder to find the diagram, he says, "Here! The diagram seems to layout everything. There is room to make things a little clearer but after knowing you all my life, well at least the part of life I remember, I know a little how your mind works."

"It's not the final product but it's best for me to get every thought down. Sam and I spent days stuck in here getting all this down. We were tired, and stuffed up on caffeinated and bad fried food, so I cannot account for all of Sam's mistakes."

"Only Sam's mistakes, right. So, beyond Sam and I, has anyone else looked at this? Perhaps people in business or tech?"

"That is what I have you and Sam for. I want Brad to be part of this too. We'll see. I'm keeping this between us for now."

"I think we will benefit from having others in from the ground floor on development. Don't you think?"

"I created this. And we have to be strategic with how we introduce Bitcoin to the people. Need to go through testing to make sure the platform is fully functioning, and everything is good. We got to take our time with this."

"I agree. You want people to know about it too. To have people looking to use, to buy, beyond just the miners, so that we have actual users as we launch. People ready to use the platform right away."

"This is not exactly the type of corporate business and money you are used to managing."

"I get that. But my experience is why you want my opinion. And I think we basically have to do some promotion for Bitcoin."

"I got to think about this. Because I don't want this to be shut down before it even gets off. Sit down with Brad and Sam too." Moto takes the binder from Sean and puts it back in the drawer. Sean eyes the drawer. "I think it might be actually helpful if I discuss this with some old associates. No specifics, just hypotheticals."

"Are you referring to the same people who are ignoring your phone calls, blocking you from getting a job?"

"You have one way of testing, which is technical. I have another way of testing the viability in the actual market. We got to be able to sell it."

Moto resumes drinking. He really didn't know what else to talk about with Sean but asks him about his future prospects. Sean didn't know what he was going to do. He also didn't know exactly what to say. But Moto's questioning made him think. "How much is each of our stakes in Bitcoin since we are partners?" He asks, "That business concept of value does not really work exactly here. A set number of Bitcoin will be given to each of us. But as explained in the binder, the value may not realize into its actual use in the market by others. Then the measures potentially can be made."

"So how many coins do I get?" Sean asks.

Moto replies, "Out of the 21 million that will ever be created, you will receive 250,000 as an initial partner. How does that sound?"

"Pretty good, Bitcoin may be my future prospects."

"No problem with that. Can always use another set of eyes working full time. It's unpaid. Sam is not being paid either to work on this, but he still has his day job. Will you be okay with that?" Moto asks, walking to the bathroom and shuts the door.

Sean jumps up and goes to the drawer. He opens the binder, flips to the red tab, and opens the binder clips. He looks back toward the bathroom and quickly takes some pages. Folds the pages and puts it in his pants pocket. Sean walks back over to the sofa, before Moto got back. Why did he just take the pages? Sean thought to himself. He didn't know why. He could have just asked Moto for them. He was a partner now anyway, so he had every right to them too. But a part of him knew he couldn't tell Moto. Moto was always so controlling of everything, couldn't see anything else. He would say no and he didn't want it to turn into an argument. And this was for Moto and the whole partnership's benefit. He would return the papers.

* * *

Sean needs this. This could save his career. Envelope in hand, inside were a copy of the pages Sean had removed from the binder. He was nervously waiting outside of Rick's office building. He didn't know if he would see him, but he was prepared for his arrival or exit out of the building. Sean spots Rick coming through the office doors, he walks to Rick.

Catching Sean heading his way, Rick picks up his phone and continues toward the elevators. His phone did not ring, and he does not dial anyone on his phone, but Rick is speaking into the phone. Sean taps Rick on the shoulder. Rick turns. "Can you hold on one second please, hey Sean how's it going?"

"Good."

"Great. I'm glad to hear that. I'm on this important call right now and running late for a meeting. Let's connect later. Okay." Rick states as he gets into the elevator. Sean follows Rick into the elevator. "I'm glad I caught you. I just wanted to follow-up on the email I sent you."

There are a few people in the elevator with them. Sean continues, "You seemed interested and I actually have a couple of others looking at this venture right now. It's news but it's the future." The elevator stops on the twelfth floor, a few people get off the elevator.

"I remember the email. Yes, I do. What have the others said about it?" Rick asks.

"Good things. But that's not what's important, what's important is this technology in the right hands with the right people like you and your firm." The elevator stops on the fifteenth floor with two people getting off.

"Autonomous, independent." The last person gets off on the nineteenth floor. Sean resumes, "Backing Bitcoin, a currency not tied to any government. Think of the possibilities."

"Not going to happen, Sean. It's time to move on."

"And how would you recommend I do that?"

"Try something new. Travel, sleep and enjoy the family. You got to figure it out. Just stop calling me and showing up at my place of business. We do not have any business with you. You are not welcome here." Rick states.

"But what about Bitcoin?"

"What about it? No, nobody is interested in your fake internet money."

Sean states, "wait, can't you just ask the boss for a meeting? I would like to speak with some of your colleagues, perhaps pitching it to your firm partners."

"I have tried to say this nicely because I do not want to hurt your feelings. But you are a liability, too risk averse, and this is a pointless proposal with no commercial value." Rick states. "Just go home" Rick presses the button to lobby before exiting the elevator.

On the elevator down, Rick's rejection hits Sean hard. Three different colleagues from reputable firms had shut Sean's elevator pitch today and Sean was just out of it. He wanted to show these firms that Bitcoin is the future. But they did not want to hear it. Perhaps they found the idea threatening to their business, something to be shutdown rather than to embrace and use for their benefit. Or they just didn't want to hear it from Sean's mouth. Being blacklisted maybe tainted everything and they could not see anything. Somehow, he had to get their attention. Sean exits the elevator and heads home.

At home, Sean just stared at the TV. After a couple hours, he substitutes the TV for his phone. Then he goes on his computer, scrolling through the news, business sites, and emails. He pulls out the papers with the diagram on blockchain technology and begins researching terms he saw. From there he begins reading blogs and messaging boards. Some people have some weird ideas and seem out of their mind. But other posts are really interesting ideas on new types of technology, and he sees how the messaging board is helping users with their development of ideas. Sean creates an account on the messaging board. He begins scanning the papers. The papers are now on his screen, ready to upload under his username. He did not click upload right away. He continues to stare at the screen, then gets up, and heads to the kitchen. Sean goes to the refrigerator, looking at the shelves one by one, but he does not choose anything. Closing the refrigerator, he walks back to the computer and clicks upload. His doorbell rings and he opens the door.

"Trick or treat!" There is a ghost, a unicorn, and a little mermaid with their baskets stretched out. He forgot to get candy and shifts in his pockets for his wallet.

"Here you go." Sean gives each a dollar. Closing the door, he walks back to the computer. He sits down, looking at the screen he cracks his knuckles and hits submit.

* * *

The blockchain technology papers have now been on the internet for a few weeks. The world is not talking about it. But Moto did hear about it, because hackers and cryptologists in the underground technology space are talking. Moto attempts to get the messaging board administrators to remove the posting of the papers, but they wouldn't. Moto should have known his attempt would be futile. He knows he can hack them. But even if the papers are removed off the messaging board, it is already out on the internet. And hundreds of people if not more, likely already copied or downloaded the papers. And those persons could share with anyone they wish.

Moto really didn't appreciate the feedback that he saw about his Bitcoin on the messaging board either and he is angry. Because he knows one of his friends had to have posted the papers. As soon as heard about the release on the messaging board, he checked his drawer for the binder. It was there. All the pages including the diagram pages were there. He had not noticed the binder being missing before. And there were only a limited number of people whom had been to his house, seen the pages and/or had access to it: Sam, Sean, and Brad. As a result, Moto cuts everyone off. No phone calls, he blocks everyone and everything. He will not speak to anyone until one of them fesses up or he figures out who did it. They are not getting anything, not one single Bitcoin.

The leak of the blockchain technology papers forces Moto to work more on his idea. He knows that he must complete the platform and launch as quickly as possible or risk someone else launching a similar platform and they're own version of Bitcoin before he can. No one is supposed to take credit for his invention, not even him. He would be damned if anyone was going to credit themselves with the inventing blockchain technology and Bitcoin. He closes himself off for months. Newspapers pile up outside, mail goes unread, knocks on his door are ignored, and his phone is silenced. A few days after New Year's, Moto launches the Bitcoin source code for the world to see.

Bitcoin: A method of payment, store of value, and medium of exchange—Virtual currency.

PART II

"*Is it perfect? No, but neither was email when it was first invented in 1972. Why should we want to build more public infrastructure? Why should we embrace blockchains over corporate intermediaries? A simple reason... Because the corporate intermediaries providing today's critical, but privately-owned infrastructure are becoming fewer, larger and more powerful, and their failures are increasingly grave.*"

—PETER VAN VALKENBURGH, COIN CENTER

CHAPTER 4

FAMILY DINNER

———

"Hey! I'm home!" said Chris.

"Did you get the garlic bread?" his wife, Lillian, asks.

He answers, "Yes!"

"From Trader, Chris?!" she asks.

"Yes!"

Lillian hears the kitchen cabinet slam.

"Where have you been?" Lillian asks.

Chris's daughter Kate rushes by him with a mouth full of lasagna and dinner plates in tow.

"Are your classes going well, Kate?" Chris asks.

"They're going. I missed you guys, Dad . . ." Kate kisses Chris on the cheek. "Who am I kidding? I'm here for the food."

"Well, we are always happy to have you. Go get your brother and tell him dinner is ready. It will be good for us to eat together as a family." Chris responds.

Kate walks to the staircase. She only gets midway before she yells for Lance to come down. She heads back downstairs and plops herself in the chair, next to her mother Lillian serving dinner. "Done!"

"Who let this one in the house? Don't you have a home?" Lance chuckles and nudges Kate, as they clamor at the table with their hands, fighting over whom gets the corner piece of the lasagna.

"Your nephew Mike is supposed to be coming over for dinner too," Lillian tells Chris.

Chris mid-chew mutters, "I have not seen him in a while either."

"He's great. You know the kids love their cousin," says Lillian.

"Is he still in school, Lillian?" asks Chris.

While preparing Chris's plate, Lillian answers, "No, last I heard he dropped out and was investing in one of those fancy Silicon Valley tech startups. You know this new generation does not understand hard work, they have it easy. You want more?"

"That's good," Chris responds.

Lillian clanks the spatula on the pan, a piece of pasta sliding off it. "Technology controls them. Don't even know how to make real friends and Facebook does not count." She looks at Lillian.

"Lillian, no phones or gadgets at the dinner table, you should be able to handle your eyes not staring at a screen for a couple of minutes and give your thumbs a rest." Chris gets the tables attention.

"Oh come on, you just don't understand," Kate interrupted. "This is just how we do things now, but our lives aren't easy. We got problems, too. Like trying to figure out how I am going to pay for graduate school, juggle my personal life, and professional career aspirations. Like everyone says, women can have it all, but can we? Like seriously, look I'm being honest, I do not know what I'm doing with my life. I have plans, but who's to say that is going to work out?"

Pushing her food around her plate with her fork, Kate continues, "I don't know if I should go into the government like you Dad or go into the private sector."

She dropped her fork on the table, released her hair from her ponytail, and ran her fingers through her hair.

She started twisting her hair into a bun while explaining, "I know I will truly have a rewarding experience with the government and I always wanted to be a civil servant, serving our country, but I need money..."

In the middle of Kate's sentence, the doorbell rings.

bbbzzzz

"Oh, that must be Mike. Hold on honey, I'll be right back." Lillian gets up from the dining table to answer the door.

"Finally, Mike is here!" Lance exclaims as he gets up from the table. "Nobody wants to hear about Kate's fake problems." Lance adjusts his voice tone to a higher pitch. "Oh, poor me, to be young and not have a brain." He continues to poke fun at Kate.

"Dad, I mean if she really got problems, Mike can help her, though." says Lance.

"And, how is that Lance?"

"Bitcoin!" Lance proclaims. "Just ask him."

"Heyyyyy, what up Mike?" Lance greets him. "How's it going?"

"I'm good, how are you?"

"You hungry, Mike?" Lillian asks.

"I can always eat, Aunt Lillian." He answers.

"Give him some air," said Chris. "Let him come in, take off his coat, and sit down."

Chris clears his throat. "Lance, what is this I hear about Silicon Valley and Bitcoin?"

"Uncle, Bitcoin is the future." Mike answers. "Thank you, auntie." Mike says to Lillian as he begins to dig into his plate.

Mike begins to tell his uncle about Bitcoin.

"Bitcoin is money, a digital currency separate from the U.S. Dollar, Euro, Chinese Yen, basically any money printed by the government. Most call it digital money. You can only use the Bitcoin on the blockchain and a few other platforms but that's okay because this is only part of it. You know." Mike says as he wipes the sauce off his face with his napkin.

Lance and Lillian are holding on to his every word. They are seated at the dining room table, family pictures surround them on the walls, the stone fireplace mantel is the center of the room, not originally part of the house, but passed down from generation to generation. Built by hand during a different time and when skills and craftsmanship was something earned, studied and valued. Chris had to have it physically moved to his home and pay extra to restore portions after installation, but it was a tie to his family, a tie to his past. His grandfather had left it for him in his will. He normally would stare at the beauty of the fireplace mantel. But all eyes were on Mike. Lance's and Lillian's eyes glisten as they exchanged smiles between ecstatic bursts of questions.

Mike continues speaking, "The way it works, is people like me agree to share our electricity and computing power to help power the platform that Bitcoin operates on. The platform is called blockchain. The platform can only function with the use of others electricity and computing power because it is the way transactions are verified, commonly referred to as proof of work. Every time I verify a transaction, I earn a Bitcoin or two, but only if I am the first to verify the blockchain transaction."

"Only if you are first?" Chris asks.

"Yes." Mike replies.

"Others who may be working to verify don't get nothing?"

"Correct, but the number of transactions even in one hour to verify are numerous, so you are bound to earn some Bitcoins." Mike answers. "Besides my primary reason is not to make money through mining but increase usage of Bitcoin as major currency, that is how the real value of Bitcoin is made. Increased usage equals increased value. Bitcoin works because there is skin in the game. If there is no skin in the game, would not really work. That is part of what makes Bitcoin unique. It rewards people who are in it, as time goes on, the value goes up."

"So how much money have you earned? Maybe you can help your favorite cousin out? I mean, share the wealth?" Lance asks.

Mike replies, "It's not super profitable to mine. I mine because I believe in it. But I have earned by virtue of increase of value of the Bitcoin I own. At this point you can only use Bitcoin in certain places but that is going to change. I have bought all types of things with Bitcoin. I have purchased baseball cap, a shirt, and my favorite hair gel. For now, you can only purchase things on certain platforms that accept the Bitcoin. But there are a bunch of things you can get, including some food orders, shipping and other services. Soon Bitcoin will be accepted everywhere. You will be able to pay for gas and your phone bill."

"This sounds cool. I'm sure all the young people think it's great but let's back up a little," said Chris.

Lance sighs, "Ignore this old man right here. Tell us more."

"Wait a minute. What if you are never able to actually use this Bitcoin in the real world? You have invested in all this time, and costs related to electricity and best technological computers, which cost money," Chris states. "Kids cannot throw their life away and savings on the hope of a big pay day or one day being able to use it in twenty years. Are there any safety protections? Do you really understand the risk?" Chris asks.

Chris is not waiting for an answer. It's not a question meant to be answered anyway. Chris is thinking out loud. Clearing the dining table of the plates and utensils, Chris states, "This may be rude, but this just sounds like a big scam. And who is the owner, CEO of this company, where are they registered?"

"Uncle, this is the beauty of the blockchain and Bitcoin. It is entirely secure and independent from any institution. Free from any bureaucracy structure. There is no CEO. There is no registration. It operates only online; it exists only because of the internet." Mike answers. Mike expects a response from his uncle Chris, but he does not respond. Mike continues speaking.

"If you can imagine the cells that make up and create your unique DNA as blocks and these blocks are building blocks, where one cannot exist without the other. This is kind of what blockchain technology does, applying the concept to money. Blockchain technology goes even further to verify the transactional history of each transaction and value, to ensure ownership of the crypto. Essentially, each transaction requires verification of where each Bitcoin came from all the way back to its initial creation on the platform and original ownership."

"Like a history log?" Chris asks.

"Exactly, building the blockchain," Mike states.

"But banks do this. So why not just continue to use my bank account to make purchases and transfers online?" Chris asks Mike.

"Well for one, we do not even need the banks. Bitcoin is digital cash working on a decentralized peer-to-peer network. There is no central bank and no single administrator. Besides, it's safer using keys."

"Keys?" Chris asks.

"Not a physical key. It's more so like a username, password function. A user gets a public key and a private key. The private key is only known by the particular user in the transaction. But the public key is verifiable through the blockchain. Trust me, no one can hack this to get your private key." Mike states.

Chris is looking at Mike. Chris states, "You don't believe me, I can tell. But I will tell you this, not even an infinite supply of electricity and computing power from the entire world would be able to get back to trace the very first original transaction of the Bitcoin, and then hack from the first transaction forward to manipulate ownership of the specific Bitcoin. This is impossible. By the time one transaction is manipulated, hundreds of additional transactions have occurred in that same time period that add on to the same blockchain. The blockchain will essentially detect by being unable to verify the history. And since its' founding (over ten years ago), there has not been one hack. The same cannot be said about our banks. Every other month there is some breach, and I get a nice, patronizing email or letter from the credit bureaus notifying me of a breach in security and that potentially my information was stolen, but it's okay and it's not their fault. Give me a break."

"Dad, he is for real." Lance states. "The value of Bitcoin is rising. It's estimated that one Bitcoin is worth $4,000.00! That is per coin!"

Mike continues talking. "Your son is right. And there are only a set number of Bitcoins in the marketplace, twenty-one million to be exact. This was done intentionally and by design by the founder of Bitcoin. This helps to stabilize the value of Bitcoin and address the pitfalls of currency deflation, especially with the use of the USD across borders in different countries, where the cost and value of the same good, service, or transaction can change in a minute. We lose money this way. And let's not even talk about all the benefits that come with eliminating the middleman costs, no more banks getting a cut for currency transfers or exchanges."

Chris's curiosity peaks. He wants better, yet he needs as much information as possible on this Bitcoin stuff. He could sit there all night with Mike and pick his brain. "Who founded Bitcoin again?"

"You have to excuse our Dad, Mike. He works for the government and tends to be a little, you know, not with the times." Kate states, her eyes shifting left to right.

"Now, the actual founder of Bitcoin is a mystery. No one truly knows. May be one person, may be a group. Many have referred to him by pseudonym. They call him Moto. That was the author name on the 2008 blockchain technology white paper."

The kids and Mike continued to carry on about Bitcoin. Mike continued to brag like a bigshot. The kids continued to fawn all over him. For years Chris had tried to get his own children excited, interested about or at the very least educated about the stock market. When their children turned fourteen years old, Lillian and Chris even bought some shares for them with a portfolio. Chris called himself teaching them about financial responsibility in a cool way, and he thought it was a cool birthday gift. Not many fourteen-year old's can brag to their friends that they own stock. He thought it was cool, he is the cool Dad. But his children never asked him one question about their stocks or how the stock market works. Their stocks essentially left to be managed under my portfolio. But he saw all this chatter from my children, wide-eyed with grins on their faces, admiring Mike.

"I want to invest," says Kate. "Dad, how about I sell my birthday stock and invest in Bitcoin?"

"With your own money that you earned, do what you want. Your mom and I bought that for you to secure your future. That is for after you graduate college, so that you have more choices to follow your passion. We want what's best for you." answers Chris.

"College cannot even guarantee me a living wage job. Every young person is going through this right now. We cannot expect anything different, as the university system is part of the institutions designed by nature to profit. They benefit primarily those with connections, access, and money. Those who do not have it, which is most, end up in debt to the system for the rest of their lives. I am not going to be a pawn in their game." Kate states.

Chris thought to himself, his children and nephew are being sold a dream. How many other children had been sold too? And this Moto, who was he?

"Uncle Chris, did you hear me?" Lance starts cheesing and takes another bite. "Can you pass the bread?" Mike taps Chris on the shoulder. But all Chris could think about is, what was the government's response? Should there be a response? Did the agency leadership know about Bitcoin? He had not heard anything. Was it a matter of the agency dropping the ball or just a matter of prioritizing? Either way, Chris felt an urgency to get to work.

* * *

The next day, Chris went into the office. He planned to raise Bitcoin at the staff meeting soon. He needed some research done on Bitcoin. Walking by one of his subordinates' desk, he asks, "Have you heard about this Bitcoin thing?" Being a recent college graduate in an entry level position, he presumed he is around the same age as his nephew and would know about it. "I can find out for you." Chris responds, "That's not what I asked. But I need you to draft a memo on the cryptocurrency, particularly on the functions of Bitcoin. I want it on my desk by the end of next week."

"Seems somewhat broad, do you have a specific legal question?" asks the subordinate.

"That is intentional. I just need you to find everything there is to know about this Bitcoin thing. I do not need you to reinvent the wheel, if there is some policy paper already analyzing this issue, summarize that and include the actual document. The important thing is to be able to understand the current state of this technology and how it exactly works." Chris answers.

"Who from upstairs is making this request?"

Chris tells him, "I am. Remember you report to me."

"Okay, I'm probably going to need to follow-up with you as I'm researching for the memo."

"I expect that. The memo should breakdown as simple as if explaining to a child. You got it?" Chris asks.

"Yes." He answers.

"I'm sorry about this. What's your name again?"

"Mitch."

"Okay Mitch" Chris walks away.

The memo produced will serve as likely an initial draft of a formal proposal to use agency resources and time to conduct an inquiry. He will have to get his department on the same page first though, and he sat down in his office to begin his own research. An internet search of Bitcoin, featured recent top news hits. Headlines raving about the emergence of crypto and in the same line stating Bitcoin had no future. Bitcoin is valued at 20,000 USD with thousands of miners and hundreds of thousands of users. A company website called BC Trusts is one of the search results and he opens it. BC Trusts only incorporated a few years ago in Delaware. "Of course." He states. Chris searches the SEC database; no registration can be found. He is surprised that it's not registered. Most trusts were publicly traded companies. Could it be just a private company? He wondered.

Scroll,

Scroll,

Scroll.

He reads, **"Transactions on the blockchain are secure in align with the company's support of user's privacy."** There are links to create a user profile and buy Bitcoin, a "How it Works" link and a "Getting Started" link. There is a FAQ page but not really much more than that. Social media pages linked on website. That is all he could look into today. Digging into Bitcoin would be a job and he have dozens of emails to get through and respond to before the endless slew of back-to-back meetings. In the "About" section on the website, there is no identification of the leadership of the company. Nothing in the news either, besides this Moto, which seemed to be an all-inclusive reference, not referred to in singular person. But a persona, character, to describe the founder in cloak of exclusivity.

Chris continues to search for Bitcoin. He sees a website on the history of Bitcoin and opens it. Browsing through the site, the usual information about a company, Chris reads, "In 2008, the vision of a purely online economy was born with Bitcoin. Bitcoin was created to function as an electronic currency that serves as payment of exchange for goods and services on the blockchain. Bitcoin's value is self-determined, independent of nominal currencies like the USD or Euro. It is a distributed public ledger on which the entire Bitcoin network relies. All transactions must be confirmed and confirmed transactions are included in the blockchain to verify ownership by the actual spender. Cryptography, essentially strong coding, reinforces the blockchain."

Chris skims through the rest, and reads, **"To have more predictability in supply there is a set number of Bitcoins in the universe, twenty million."** He continues to browse through the website.

Wait a minute, he knows what to do. Chris picks up the phone and dials a colleague in Justice that works in the computer crimes division. He gets to handle the crimes committed on the dark-net. He has all the fun with setting up sting operations on the web, network intelligence techniques, wiretaps, and complete carte blanche. If anyone knows about Bitcoin and crypto, he would. Anonymous transactions on the web with no useful paper trail to prove identity was Justice worst nightmare come true. Criminal's inevitability will try to exploit. When Chris finally gets a hold of his contact at Justice, he was told the CFTC (Commodity and Future's Trading Commission) had briefed Justice on Bitcoin a few months ago. The information was subject to an ongoing investigation, so not too much could be revealed, as the information was disclosed only on a need-to-know basis. A bunch of security clearance jargon and agency jurisdiction rambled out of his mouth. Bells in my head went off as soon as the letters C-F-T-C were said. The CFTC had already made moves to exert authority in this area. "Yeah, thanks. Inter-agency collaboration seems promising and requires share of any information possible."

Chris will send a formal request to the CFTC with the pleasantries. But Chris will be buying his time until he receives the memo and can hopefully get the full backing of the agency heads from upstairs. During the week, Chris will inquire on the progress of the memo. Discussions pouring over documents, the memo was taking shape. Beyond the Bitcoin and blockchain technology functions, the agency also needed to understand if Bitcoin was a security. If yes, what should be the required disclosures? Perhaps disclosure on operations and procedures. And what are the safeguards against fraud or misuse to protect investors? Chris learns that any attempt to hack would require the hacker to redo the entire proof-of-work on the block and all blocks after it on the blockchain, and then catch up with and surpass the work of the legitimate transactions occurring and being confirmed in real-time.

* * *

A week later, the memo is on Chris' desk. Attached to the memo is also a white paper on Bitcoin. Not produced by Bitcoin itself, but a group of computer coders and cryptographers dedicated to code development to improve the platform. Reviewing the memo, it was clear that Bitcoin by design is to evade government regulation. As the white paper explained, "the electronic system is based on cryptographic proof" of ownership, not assurance of ownership based on the trust in another, this trust traditionally was shown and/or proven through credit that is backed by a bank or financial institution. These institutions are subject to extensive government regulation and information collection procedures.

The afternoon staff meeting is in a few hours, and while he did not submit any agenda items, he plans to push the Bitcoin issue at the end of the meeting. Chris calls Mitch into his office to review the memo in detail. As they go through the memo, point-by-point, he remembers that he has yet to hear back from the CFTC. "Get the CFTC Chairman on the line for me." He tells Mitch.

Mitch calls a contact at the CFTC, Joe Mieja. Mitch starts talking to Joe, "Hey Joe. How's it going? I really just need to be put in direct contact with the CFTC Chairman."

Chris is standing in front of Mitch waiting. He is watching Mitch.

"Sure, no problem. Let me see if he is available. Hold on." Joe states. Mitch is put on hold, elevator music plays. After a few minutes, Joe comes back on the phone, "He's not able to talk right now. But says if it's about anything crypto he can talk to me."

Mitch responds to the SEC Chairman, "His deputy investigators say he is unavailable, but he is happy to schedule an appointment for you with the Chairman later. He also says he is the best person to speak to about cryptocurrency and the Chairman would direct you to him anyway. So, he is available to talk. His name is Joe Mieja."

"Mieja! I want the chairman, not his assistant. Let's just go!" Chris tells Mitch. Mitch tells Joe they will have to call back him back.

So now Chris is walking into the staff meeting, preparing to propose an inquiry into the jurisdiction of the SEC over Bitcoin and the legality of the cryptocurrency platforms, with no inter-agency cooperation. Chris walks into the conference room with Mitch. He sits down, but Mitch stands. The most senior employees are around the table, while others stand.

Chris's supervisor begins the meeting, "Okay guys, we got a full agenda, let's begin."

One by one, agency division leads provide updates on case load and investigation status of select priority matters. Confidential information is shared, agency testimony for upcoming hearings and briefings are discussed, research tasks are assigned, and entry level staff is ferociously taking notes. Recommendations for new and renewed agency rulemaking are proposed. There is back and forth chatter. The bureaucracy wheels are churning slowly.

Chris' supervisor continues to facilitate the meeting, "Next. Report on the Brazilian whistle-blower case."

Chris' colleague began to present his report, passing out a copy of the summary of the report. He briefly went through the facts. Some was reported in the news, but the case was dependent upon the credibility of the whistle-blower. The presenter is discussing anti-corruption practices or the lack thereof in the case. The legal recourse was available potentially under U.S. law and Brazilian law. The whistle-blower testimony was crucial in turning what would be lower level defendants into cooperating witnesses against the company leadership. Chris is reviewing his talking points. Papers, including the memorandum and note pad are highlighted.

"Great job, any updates, proposals or issues, not on the agenda anyone would like to raise?"

Chris states, "Yes I do."

"Okay, go ahead."

"Most of us are aware that there is an entire separate commerce market on the internet. Now some of you may have heard about Bitcoin. Bitcoin is its own currency for the online market, independent from nominal currency like the USD or Euro. Uniquely, Bitcoin, a digital currency can be used to pay for goods as well as services and exchange in transactions. Not linked to a bank or financial institution.

People can earn, buy, and/or transact in this currency. Transactions are verified by the blockchain." Chris begins to draw on the smart board. Drawing three rectangles side by side, pointing to the first rectangle, he continues to describe blockchain "Each rectangle represents a block. Each transaction from the original transaction is time stamped and assigned a unique hash number." Pointing to the first block. "As later blocks are chained after it." Chris is connecting the first block to the second block with a pointing arrow. "In order to verify the current transaction that is taking place in block 3, the transactions in both blocks 1 and 2 are verified. This is known as proof of work." Chris connects the second block to the third block. "Every transaction is stored into the blockchain. Attempts to hack it, to steal Bitcoin, will require each individual block to be changed that is associated with the Bitcoins work to change each. This is impossible."

"Excuse me Chris," a colleague says. "What does this have to do with the SEC?"

"Investors are also joining in on this Bitcoin mania, buying and selling digital currency. The value of Bitcoin is rising, so we expect the number of investors to increase. This of course raises red flags for the SEC. There is a thin line from where users cross into being users and investors. Users and investors are vulnerable to being taken advantage of by an exciting technology with no disclosure reporting on risk. There is a lack of information on how this thing works. The CFTC is already looking into Bitcoin."

"Chris, what drives people to Bitcoin?" asks a SEC investigator.

"The youth are hoping to cash in and make some money mining Bitcoin, using their computing power and electricity to verify transactions on the blockchain when a new transaction occurs."

A colleague asks, "Wait, the CFTC has authority?"

"The law again here is not exactly clear. But, even where CFTC may have jurisdiction, that does not take away from the SEC's jurisdiction, a crypto asset for all intensive purposes, there is an expectation of profit from the investment made based on the entrepreneurial or managerial efforts of others, offering a security, could be subject to both CFTC and SEC at the same time. It truly will take an individual assessment on a case-by-case basis, legal analysis of how the entity functions, design framework, nature of transaction, and expectation of the investor." Chris replies.

Chris's boss cuts in, "Okay. We need to discuss further at another time. Let's table this to next week."

"I think we have to do something. This must be a policy priority. This cannot wait another week. It will just get pushed off to endless cycle of deferral." Chris responds.

"We cannot make a decision at this time. Like all policy decisions we have to exercise diligence. You know this Chris. I am glad you raised this issue and it is important. We will circle back and take it from there," his supervisor states.

The staff meeting ends. Chris heads back to his office. Chris yells over to Mitch, "Get in here!"

"Yes, Mr. Donaldson." Mitch states, rushing into Chris's office.

"We have to get more to convince them this is a priority. We need more than this memorandum. So, what are you thinking? How we do this?" Chris asks.

"We investigate and insert ourselves so that the agency is forced to address the issue." Mitch replies.

"We don't have any investigations tied to Bitcoin right now. That's what I'm trying to get the agency to give us the resources to do." Chris states.

"Maybe it doesn't have to be an official SEC investigation. We can continue to poke around, monitor the media reports on Bitcoin." Mitch responds.

Chris tells Mitch, "Get Joe Mieja on the line now! We are going to partner with him on whatever is going on at the CFTC on this. He did say I can talk to him about crypto."

"You want me to transfer him over to your phone?" Mitch asks.

"No, ask him to meet." Chris directs Mitch.

"I'm on it!" Mitch answers and leaves Chris's office. He dials Joe. Joe answers the phone and Mitch asks him, "Mr. Mieja how do you feel about discussing crypto over coffee?"

CHAPTER 5

CRYPTO WINTER

———

Stretching out on his canopy overlooking the ocean, Moto takes in all the sun. The bungalow has everything he needs. The wood seems to capture the cool air from the night as his feet were cold the minute, he took off the sheets. There was no sleeping in. His body is in Samoa, but it is still running on Cali work schedule. No meetings, no calls, nothing. Not even a trip itinerary. He thought about exploring the islands but that would ruin it. He liked his space and he already have the best view of Samoa, breathtaking.

He walks into his bungalow to the kitchen and picks some fruit from the fruit plate left in his room. The mango is fresh and apples crisp. It never fails. Next to the fruit plate was a note, undoubtedly left by the staff when they brought in breakfast. The note read, "We have picked out some great excursions for solo vacationers, both outdoor adventures as well as places to socialize to get the most out of your stay. We are here for all your solo travel needs."

Solo travel is all Moto can do at this point. He didn't want anyone around. He doesn't trust anyone.

Moto did not forget about the release of his blockchain paper on the internet and he knows one of them did it and he will not forget. Moto was betrayed by a friend, maybe one of them or maybe all. But betrayal is betrayal, no matter how big or how many involved. And he refused to reward them either. The plan was to give a share of Bitcoins to Brad, Sean, and Sam, like he with Lars upon launch, but that went out the window with the betrayal. And when he decided that none of them would receive any Bitcoins from him in its initial release, he meant it. If they wanted Bitcoin, they would have to mine it and earn it or buy it like everyone else.

Moto tracked down the username that posted the paper on the messaging board to the IP address of the computer used. He can narrow the location of the computer used to an area within a fifteen-mile radius of the center of San Francisco. All of them, Brad, Sean, and Sam lived in that area. But Moto only suspected Sean and Sam, because they are the only ones who had been in his home and knew where he kept the Bitcoin white paper. Moto had just sought Brad's legal advice.

Moto mainly suspected Sean, Sam had a job and was not really counting on Bitcoin to be successful to make money. He was really just intrigued by all the technical things and seeing it actually work. Moto missed those conversations and game nights. Moto refused to attend any, but Sam always invited him. Sam even came to him with the offer to be a partner in a new venture, BC Trusts. Moto agreed on three conditions. First, that Moto is a silent partner. Second, that Moto is the only partner with Sam. And third, BC Trusts is not to own more than 1% of all Bitcoin in circulation and ownership is held by the company, not individual associates, partners, or board members. Moto demanded the third condition on a whim because Sam initially wanted all of them, Sam, Brad, Sean, and Moto to be partners, but with Moto's second condition, would settle on Sean and Brad being on the board in more of an advisory capacity.

Moto's bet was on Sean. That Sean did it, stole his white paper on blockchain and posted it on the internet. Sean was too eager to see Bitcoin on the market and quickly. He kept pushing Moto, and even now always pushing on him that Bitcoin is a business and we got to capitalize mumble jumble. He out of everybody did not get it. He wouldn't think twice about the impact and Moto's real purpose on creating Bitcoin. It was all just business. Plus, Moto remembers that around that time Sean had just lost his job and that is why he wanted to be involved in Bitcoin. Sean always felt like he knew better than anyone else because of his MBA and job. But once that was gone, that shield was gone and maybe he broke. Moto did not know, and he did not care. Sean was wrong and Moto did not need to be crossed twice.

*** * ***

He got up early one morning, determined to hunt his own dinner. Maybe he was trying to prove something to himself. He rented a boat and was out there in the little boat for hours. He came back empty handed and was frustrated. He thought maybe he should have just rented a tour with one of the local fishery companies. But he quickly pushed that idea out of his mind. He was more than just some Cali guy good with numbers. Anyway, he had to feed himself and decided that after two weeks maybe it was time to travel the dock back to land. From there he could head downtown. The concierge had recommended quite a few restaurants in the city for dinner. He only had a few more nights here he should at least go out once.

His cab driver sparks up a conversation, "Hey, where you from?"

"California." Moto answers.

"I hear it's hot there. I've never been to the United States but if I were to go, California is one of the places I would go. I have had quite a few riders from California here on vacation. Where you headed?" The cab driver asks.

"The hotel recommended Samoan BBQ. It's supposed to be local food with some BBQ. Can't go wrong with that." Moto replies.

"Okay. Good choice. There is also a bar next door. My friend owns the spot. Real cool vibes to go to after dinner." The cab driver states.

"What's it called?" Moto asks.

"Pete's Bar." Cab driver answers.

"A lot of tourists?" Moto asks.

"It's a mix." Cab driver replies.

"Thanks. Do you have any other recommendations?" Moto asks.

"Yes. I know quite a few spots, depending on your taste. If you're in the mood for something light, fresh fish and stuff, go to Ma's Shack. If you want some American food go to Sue's Place. I believe there is also a Chinese food place next door." The driver responds.

"How long is the drive there?" Moto asks.

"Fifteen or twenty minutes." The driver answers.

"Everywhere is twenty minutes. That is the same time the cab driver from the airport told me," Moto states.

"Yeah, everything is pretty much in the center of the island, and its twenty minutes to the center," the cab driver states.

Moto stares out the window. He feels every bump and curve in the road. "It's dark. There are very few streetlights. How do people drive at night?"

"All we need is the car light. That's enough. Plus, there are more lights as you get closer to town." Cab driver answers Moto.

Moto turns his head and looks out the back window and says, "It's pitch black, that can't be safe."

"We're used to it." Cab driver replies.

"Hmm, okay." Moto says. "I can easily catch a cab there to come back up?" Moto asks.

"Yeah, no problem." Cab driver replies.

* * *

Moto is really enjoying the BBQ. He did not know what they put in the sauce but there is a secret ingredient to the recipe. The sauce would make anything taste good. He could not even remember the last time he ate actual meat. Everyone is vegan back home, and everything is always about the hip new vegan cuisine. The vegan restaurants were great, and he planned to maintain his healthy lifestyle. But this was vacation and he deserved a cheat meal.

He finished his plate and took care of the check. After tipping the waitress, he thought he would stop by Pete's Bar for a drink. Beyond the hotel employees and taxi drivers, Moto did not have any human contact in a while. The purpose of the trip was to get a break and to cut himself off from the world, but he wanted to drink, and while Samoan BBQ could cook a tasty pork, their drinks were lackluster.

Moto entered the bar next door. Pete's Bar is a change of pace. It is lively. Moto walked around freely with space to choose a seat at the bar or a table. He could see people socializing in the back.

"Excuse me. Do you mind?"

"Sir? Excuse me." Moto repeats himself to the customer, a man scrolling through his phone.

"Someone sitting here?" Moto asks the man at the bar again.

"Not at all, sorry. Yeah, no one is sitting there." The man finally replies.

Moto takes a seat at the bar and speaks to the bartender. "Hello. Jack please. Straight."

"You want to open a tab?" asks the bartender.

"Sure, here you go." The bartender takes Moto's card.

Moto waiting for his drink looks around the bar. The man next to him is staring at his phone reading.

"Here you go." The bartender places the glass in front of Moto. Moto takes a drink.

"Oh lord this is crazy." the man states. Moto turns his head, "people who invested in this are about to lose their minds." The man states and looks up briefly to take a sip from his glass. "I would be pissed." The man continues.

"People invested in what?" Moto asks.

"You haven't heard the news?" the man questions.

"Nothing good comes from the news. I stopped reading newspapers a long time ago." Moto responds.

"I hear that. Well, a lot of people lost a lot of money today, the latest victims in a scam of millions, same old story. Company was trusted to keep their customer's money safe and the company ran off with all the money, all gone." The man replies.

"What company?" Moto asks.

"Some online thing, weird name too." The man looks back at his phone, fingers moving down the screen. "Ah. I found it. Mt. X", he states.

"Mt. X?" Moto asks.

"You know the company? You heard of it?" The man takes a sip of his drink.

"You sure that's the name?" Moto responds.

"Yea, that's what it says." the man states.

"Can I see that?" Moto asks the man.

"My phone?" The man asks.

"Uhhh, yeah." Moto answers.

The man responds, "You know you can just look it up online on your phone."

"Ah, yeah. I'm sorry, the thing is that I do not have my phone. I actually surprised myself, the place I am staying at is part of this whole phone free zone, promoting this whole social media thing, detoxing from the online world, and trying the whole inner peace thing." A million things are going through his head right now, but he manages a chuckle.

"Okay." The man slides the phone toward Moto. Moto waves the bartender over, "Can you get this guy another one on me." Moto begins to read the article.

"Don't run with my phone." The man laughs. Moto turns to him, smirks quickly, and looks back to the phone. "What the fuck?" Moto states out loud. "No, they did not, bankruptcy? The oldest trick in the book." The man interjects, "Yeah man." He puts his glass down on the bar.

As Moto keeps reading, he grows more concerned. Millions of Bitcoin just went missing, and the owners of Mt. X claimed to not know where the bitcoin had gone. Apparently, the bitcoin was stolen over a period of years, 850,000 bitcoins.

"Shit!" Moto exclaims.

The value of Bitcoin was steady rising and gaining traction in the finance industry, but now everything he created could be in jeopardy.

"You okay?" The man asks.

"Yea. Yea. Yea." Moto responds.

"Did you invest in that thing?" The man asks him.

"Not exactly." Moto answers the man.

"Damn. Well either way man, I'm sorry." The man says to Moto.

Moto continues to read. In the time that Moto had been on the island, bankruptcy papers had been filed by Mt. X. Followed by a leak to the news of the missing bitcoins, multiple lawsuit filings for fraud, and a class action. There would be a ripple effect. He opens a new browser and searches bitcoin. At the top of the list is "Bitcoin plummets: Valued at $300 for now."

Moto's right leg is shaking. He knew Sam, as his partner, and the board were underwater. They probably have been trying to reach him on his cell, which he had turned off, and he did not tell anyone where he would stay. He had to go. Moto nearly knocks over the stool getting up, stumbles slightly.

"Your card sir. Close the tab?" The bartender asks Moto.

"Yes. I almost forgot." stuffing his credit card in the pocket of his jeans.

"Geez man, you're in a hurry suddenly. You don't have to be rude, could say thank you." The man says.

Moto cuts his eye at the man, and says "Don't do that, man, that is what the drink was for."

The man sucks his teeth, grabs his phone. He sees the bitcoin search on his phone. He looks up, looking for Moto. But Moto is gone. "Damn man. That sucks," the man states followed by a straight shot of jack.

Moto is outside the bar. He does not see any cabs. And now the nighttime scene inside Pete's Bar seems a little deserted to Moto. Samoan BBQ is closed. Just exactly how long had he been inside the bar? It could not have been too long. He didn't have a watch. He was looking at that man's phone the entire time and did not look at the time. Or maybe restaurants just closed early here. He went back inside the pub and asked the bartender to call him a cab.

Heading back, this time he was anticipating every curve and bump. Counting each one and growing more and more impatient. It was taking forever to get back.

"Do you mind driving a little faster?" Moto asks.

"I don't want to go too fast Sir. Not a lot of lights out here." the driver states.

No more curves. The road is less bumpy now. A sign they finally reached the resort area. Resorts line the coast, along the same direction of the road to his right.

"Are we almost there?" Moto asks the driver.

"Just a few more minutes. Not long." The cab driver states.

He sees lights in the distance. Silence and then ten, maybe fifteen minutes go by when they catch up to the lights. As they approach, Moto tells the driver, "This is it, right up here."

The driver responds, "I don't think so Sir. You are staying at Bungalow and Villas. That is the Villas. Tourists confuse them all the time. They need to change the name. Design is the same too. Both used to be owned by the same family about ten years ago. They're from the island. But they sold the land a few years back or so to some developer. I think he is British. I don't know. They all start to look alike after a while. You know? The family also ..."

Moto interrupts, "please just stop talking."

"I'm sorry, didn't mean to make you angry." The driver says and stares at the road.

"I just need some peace and quiet. I'm sorry." Says Moto.

The driver nods, not taking his eyes off the road. But the rest of his face is expressionless.

Silence.

Right up the road, there are more lights. This time it is his hotel. The taxi turns into the roundabout, entering the driveway to the resort front desk reception.

Moto hands the driver twenty dollars and jumps out of the car.

Back at his bungalow, Moto fumbles through his luggage for his phone. He turns on his phone and calls Sean. The automatic message plays, "The number you dialed is not accepting phone calls at this time. Please hang up and try your call again later." He redials again. He hears the same message. He checks his settings to make sure data roaming was on and the international capability was on. He redials again and again and again. But his phone apparently cannot connect fully to a signal. He goes outside the bungalow, the phone in his hand, looking for a signal, anywhere. He rushes across the dock to the hotel desk on land, still searching for a signal. "Shit this damn, fucking place."

"Excuse me. This is kind of an emergency. I need to reach someone back in the United States. Is there any Wi-Fi I can use? I'll pay for it, no problem." Moto asks the lady at the front desk.

"Are you okay sir? Do you need a doctor?" The receptionist asks.

"No, I'm fine. I just need to make a phone call." Moto responds.

"I'm sorry Sir. No, we do not. These are internet-free spaces. None of the villas or bungalows have internet in accordance with providing a tranquil environment free from outside pressures. You can borrow my phone to make local calls if you like, or I can have the concierge arrange for a taxi to take you downtown to an internet cafe or to a store where they sell international calling cards." the receptionist states.

Looking through the phone settings, messing with every function, he resets the phone and heads back to his bungalow. He powers off the phone. Back at his room, he takes out the battery and sim to help the phone reboot. "Maybe this will help get a signal." A couple of minutes later, his phone is back on, still no signal. "Fuck!" Moto slams his fist on the table, goes outside of the bungalow to the water and threw his phone, "piece of shit."

He begins to gather all his belongings in the bungalow. Throwing things in the suitcase, he hastily packs up, grabs his suitcase and heads to the front desk.

"I need a cab and I'm checking out." Moto states to the receptionist.

"Of course, sir, I will get one right away for you. Where are you going?"

"To the airport" Moto responds.

Moments later the cab arrives. "Okay sir, the cab is here. And everything is already settled by the bank. Thank you for staying with Samoan Bungalows and Villas. And visit us again." the lady at the front desk smiles. Moto walks away.

It was the same driver from the other night and he eagerly greeted Moto. "How are you my friend? Are you leaving us?"

"Yes. I have to go." Moto states.

Moto got in the backseat and when the driver shut the trunk, a new sense of urgency overcame him. Moto began tapping his feet and playing with his fingers.

"Sir, let me know if you would like me to open the windows back there. I don't leave them open because I never know when there will be a little rain on the island. I don't want you to get wet. We are used to it, but let me know if you need some air," says the cab driver.

"About how long until we get to the airport?" asks Moto.

"Oh, we will be there in no time, about twenty minutes or so, maybe less. Don't worry about it, I'll get you to your flight." the driver said.

"I just need to get back to the States." Moto responds.

"Don't worry. How did you enjoy your stay with us?" The cab driver asks.

"Sir, not now."

When he woke up today, he thought it was any other Wednesday. This is not what Moto envisioned or set out to do. The darknet was corrupting a very good idea. The coup of a noble cause and there was little Moto could do.

* * *

Lars picks up Moto from airport arrivals. Moto opens the car door and gets in the front passenger seat. Cars are honking, as Lars speeds off.

"Hey." Lars says to Moto.

"Hey." Moto grumbles.

"How was your trip back?" Lar asks.

"It was fine." Moto answers. "Thanks for picking me up too, Lars."

"Yeah, no problem. We are right around the corner from the office, I'm surprised you just didn't take a cab." Lars responds.

"I really didn't want to deal with anyone. Have not had a good experience with cab drivers lately." Moto replies.

"Oh." Lars states. "But beyond the obvious, how is everything else? You have been away for a while, how is the vaca? Island living?" Lars asks.

Moto answers, "I took a step back after the Bitcoin white paper in 2008. It's been three years now. I'm not trying to be involved like that. That is why I am a silent partner, you know. It's frustrating to see how Bitcoin has been used."

Lar responds, "Well you know that is outside your control."

Moto states, "It's not about that, about having control or anything. The thing is that more things should have been anticipated with Bitcoin competing with the U.S. dollar, there would all these other similar coins created to try to advantage of it, but in a way where trading off a lot of privacy and freedom."

Lars responds, "But what you did, with Bitcoin is amazing. Those other coins, tokens, whatever, can be shut down any day by the government. Bitcoin cannot be shut down."

"Yeah, I know, but . . ."

Lars interrupts Moto, "But nothing. You did more than enough and even if you cannot see it now. You have and will help so many people across the world. You may never know them, and they will never know you, but just be sure of your contribution to society."

"None of coins not even Bitcoin will address inequality, but Bitcoin will address equality of opportunity. You don't need to prove yourself, don't need bank account or proof of identity (major issues to access in unbanked population). All you need is a phone or internet. By the end of next year 6 billion people will have a phone and access to the internet. This is a permissionless way to get access with no government involvement." Moto states.

Lar signals left and looks at Moto, "we are almost there now."

"I know. Don't remind me. I got to deal with this mess now." Moto states.

"You know, I am here for you. Call me anytime." Lar states, pulling up to the office building.

"I'm call you later." Moto opens the car door and proceeds upstairs to BC Trusts. He goes up in the elevator to the office and walks directly pass the receptionist, not saying a word to Sean's office and waits.

"What the fuck?" Moto states to Sean, as he opens his office door.

"Well good morning to you too Moto." Sean replies. "You're in my office," He states.

Sean pauses and takes a deep breath. He takes a seat next to Moto and puts his hand on Moto's shoulder. Sean continues speaking.

"I tried to call you. We all did. Where have you been?" Sean asks.

"Yeah, I was out of range in Samoa and got a new phone too. I heard about Bitcoin plummet and I came back as soon as I heard." Moto responds. He drops his bag on the side of his desk.

"What has Sam done so far? And where is Sam? I stopped at his office first, he wasn't there," Moto states.

"I don't know where Sam is, probably on his way in. It's not like we keep office hours. I was in there waiting on him too." Sean states.

"Why in his office?" Moto questions Sean.

"He has a better view." Sean responds.

"Sean, don't enter my office without my permission." Moto tells him.

Sean laughs. "Whatever man, you got it."

"I'm serious Sean, respect boundaries," Moto states.

Sean laughs and shakes his head. He stays put in his chair and has no intent on leaving.

"Since you're here, what steps have you guys discussed to lessen the damage?" Moto asks Sean.

"The PR damage is a nightmare." Sean responds. "But nothing we can't get over, just going to ride it out. Sean wanted to issue a press statement, but Brad advised against it, can't have an interpretation that we are acknowledging guilt or wrongdoing." Sean states.

"Well what do you know about what happened? Why did the value of Bitcoin drop so much so quickly?" Moto asks.

"Just what the news is reporting. Government interviews and press statements." Sean answers. "My guess is that once people started seeing it fall, they began to panic and sell at a lower value than even the market price. And set off a ripple effect, happens on Wall Street." Sean states.

"That still doesn't tell me what has been done and what we are going to do," Moto states.

"What are we going to do?" Sean chuckles.

"You cannot be serious." Sean shakes his finger. "I'll tell you what we are going to do. Nothing! We had nothing to do with it. People can blame only themselves, not us. They trusted the wrong person with money. It's messed up. I get that. But we are not, you hear me, not responsible!" Sean states.

"I can't talk to you. Sam and I will figure out how this happened and what do," Moto states.

"For what? I know the value of bitcoin has gone down. A lot, I have some assets I can make liquid if you need something. It may take some time but I'm here for you. The whole team is here for..."

Moto interrupts Sean. "This is bad for BC Trusts."

"People are going to want to take their Bitcoin out of our holdings. We can take a hit if we don't do this strategically. I suggest a personal touch. We have to call our biggest account holders first and smooth things over. Sit down, all of us, when Sam and Brad get in, go over each of the biggest account holder's needs, likes, and dislikes. We then assign each account holder call to one of us based on which of us can tap into the unique needs and wants of the account holder and persuade them to stay with us. I think it's only fair that the person who brought the account holder in as an account for the company get default. The Peterson account is definitely mine. You can handle Henderson if you like. I think I'll mess that one all up with prior employment disagreements." Sean finishes speaking.

Moto is staring at Sean. "Are you done? Is that all you think we should care about right now? People are losing everything right now! This is not about me, not about you, or this company. Sean, think about what I created. Bitcoin is bigger than this company. Just when Bitcoin becomes mainstream, this shit happens. Too convenient, something is not right. We need to dig. Find out what happened at Mt. X, how they did it and why. All the players need to be looked at," Moto states.

"They did it for the money. It's that simple Moto. You always think there is something bigger, you and your conspiracy theories." Sean responds.

Moto stares intently at Sean and says, "And exactly what the fuck is that supposed to mean?"

Sean replies, "Ford Hall."

Moto crosses his eyes at Sean. Seeming a little vexed, Sean heads to the door. "Go home to your wife Sean," says Moto. Sean slams the door.

"Ford Hall," Moto grumbles reclining back. He could never forget Ford Hall.

He remembers it was a Friday in December when Ford Hall happened. Nearly ten years ago, a group of students came together to discuss the rising student debt they all faced. We had already petitioned the university president and organized meetings to negotiate lower interest rates, interest forgiveness where the original loan amount paid off in ten years from graduation, and increasing paid fellowship and residential assistant opportunities, and scholarship awards. We felt like we were making progress. But at the same time, we were having meetings and protests with the administration, so was CA Bank.

They were in bed with each other and we knew it but could not prove it. We knew that CA Bank was the university's bank, and largest supplier of credit to the university to keep the university's necessities functioning. The university was not paying CA Bank back this credit or the interest on the credit. And the bank was not seeking to enforce payment, just continued extensions and increases in lines of credit. Leaked documents a few years after I graduated showed an understanding between the university and CA Bank that credit to the university would be guaranteed as long as CA Bank was the number one recommended bank for students to secure private loans to cover tuition costs and school expenses, and twenty-five percent of all university students in need of additional aid applied for a private loan from CA Bank.

There were compromises made by the group with the administration, too many in my opinion. I believe this is what gave the administration the ammunition to be able to divide and conquer with individual promises to those students who were persuadable. These students weren't the organizers of the protest, merely supporters and followers. When they no longer had a personal stake, they went right on to following the administration. And this is how we fell. Like the frantic gasps for air of a person drowning, that is when we took Ford Hall.

There was no going back after that, for no one. And even now, the 7 days in Ford Hall, a move of sheer desperation, showed the power of the people.

Knock.

Knock.

Sam finally arrives. He enters Moto's office with Sean and sits next to him.

"We were just talking about you Sam." Sean states.

"Good to see you back Moto." Sam tells him. "How was your vacation?" Sam asks Moto.

"It was good. Cut a little short, got to do it again." Moto responds to Sam.

"Mt. X, the reason we are all here." Sam states.

"I was telling Moto that we agreed to not get involved. Keep our names out of. It's the market, these things happen. We are not responsible; we didn't tell those people to sell or buy Bitcoin." Sean states to Sam.

"I disagree with Sean, you and I have to decide the best course of action to respond. We have to respond. We are a leader in the crypto market. We must use it to help and find proactive steps to keep it. I was thinking about issuing like a one-page guidance on trading, selling and buying, and market fluctuations, or maybe sending out an update on our cyber security procedures, hosting an online town hall for our account holders to ask questions. We need to do something, not just hide and twiddle our thumbs." Moto tells Sam.

"Can you excuse us Sean, give Moto and I the room." Sam states.

Sean leaves Moto's office.

"I spoke with Brad when this all first happened. And it is his legal opinion that we tread carefully for liability purposes and I agree. I don't think any of your recommendations would raise any issue but want to give some time for Brad to review your recommendations. I agree with you too that we got to do something," Moto states.

"Is Brad coming in today?" Moto asks Sam.

"He should be. But he probably got his hands full advising his personal clients." Sam answers.

"Thank you for coming back. I need you here with all this. Your perspective keeps us, well at least me, leveled.

You know sometimes Sean and Brad can get consumed and lose sight of the big picture. But you should go home and drop your luggage and things off. Then come back in this afternoon and we can all talk. Brad should be in and Sean hopefully, my fingers crossed, won't be wound so tight." Sam says and laughs.

"I'm not going home now. For what, would just be wasting time, I can unpack and do all of that stuff later. I'm staying here to get some work done, catch up on emails, market news, and price analysis." Moto smiles and turns in his chair. "Just getting a head start on the research for those recommendations," Moto responds.

Sam gets up to leave. "Sam?" Moto gets his attention. "I can't be home in my house with no worries, when some people have lost their life savings, retirement, everything. I feel an obligation. You know. You understand right?" Moto tells Sam.

Sam replies, "I know Moto, I know."

CHAPTER 6

BUYER BEWARE

Mike is heading to the grocery store, stacking up on his snacks for a long night of mining, maybe some coding, and a game or two. Recently, Mike had been thinking about his future, cashing in on his Bitcoin through a crypto exchange, opening a business, or maybe moving to a new city.

Mike walks into his house and commands his virtual assistant, "Sue turn game console on." "Turning console on and you have four messages." "Sue is MLead88 online." "Yes, MLead88 is online." "Send request to join me on the game."

Mike logs into the game room. MLead88 joins him. They begin to play. Mike and MLead88 are teamed up in the game against two other players.

"Hey what's up bro?" Mike fumbles to put his game headset on.

"Good. How's it going?" MLead88 replies.

"Good. You just getting on?" Mike asks.

"Yea had to do the 9-5 gig."

"I don't know how you do it man." Mike says.

"I can't hear you clearly. You got your mic on?" MLead88 replies.

Mike checks his headset. He presses "x" on the controller. Splits the screen and opens setting to check his headset connection and his mic volume. "Yo, you hear me?"

"Yeah."

"Yo get him. Over there, he's on your left man, heading to the forest. I don't know how you do the 9 to 5 thing." Mike states.

"Ok, I see him." MLead88 replies.

"Yeah, you know I got to have the finer things in life. Like food, a bed, a roof. You know the best." MLead88 laughs.

Mike laughs. "On your right, yo, yo, yo watch out."

"Yea, I got him. Thanks." MLead88 replies.

Mike continues. "Got you. Yeah, yeah, he is going up the bank, right above you. Meet me under the cliff." Mike says in the mic.

"Shit, yeah, I've been meaning to talk to you about this Bitcoin stuff. I think you mentioned something about it before." MLead88 replies.

"Yeah, what do you want to know?" Mike asks.

"I was curious about how it works. You know I've been thinking about investing in this company that allows people to basically change their Bitcoin into cash." MLead88 states.

"What's it called?" Mike asks.

MLead88 replies, "Bitcoin Investments. You know them?"

"Nah. But Bitcoin is kind of a sure thing. How did you find this company?" Mike states.

"A couple of the gamers on here have been talking about it," MLead88 states.

"I met this guy. He's also a gamer on here. Jones, his game handle on here is Private67. I don't know if you know him, gamed with him on here. He's cool. An entrepreneur started this company a couple months ago, you know. Been doing well so far, have talked to a couple people that have invested their Bitcoin with his company and they are making money off the investment. You know I value your opinion. You know more about this thing than me. This is what you do. I'm interested, and I don't want to regret not investing, like damn man, everybody making money and I could have made some too. You, know?" MLead88 says.

"I tell everybody, the most money I have ever made is with Bitcoin. I can invite him to join us on here and we can all chat. You know all the questions to ask." Mike tells MLead88.

"That's cool. You need to know what the risk is and estimated growth. Those are the basics, picked that up from my former college days.""

"What's your name by the way?" Mike asks.

MLead88 replies, "Mitch."

* * *

Over the next few weeks, Mike speaks with Mitch and Jones. They discuss Bitcoin Investment LLC, crypto assets and Bitcoin. They would often text each other links to articles about the Bitcoin market. They chatted usually on the game console. They never got a chance to meet in person, so when Mitch suggested meeting Mike at Barnes and Noble, Mike knew it was a sign that Mitch was likely on board with the Bitcoin Investments. They decided on a public place for meeting, lessening Mitch's concerns. Even though they have talked for months they are strangers. He didn't think Mitch was dangerous; but he knows that people can be capable of things least expected. He knows Mike didn't work, and in the current state of the world, crazy things happen every day, he could be getting set up. Thankfully, everything turned out fine. Mike and Mitch met with no problems. They continued to talk; and Mitch agreed to meet Jones in person.

Mike took Mitch downtown to see Jones. They went to the Bitcoin Investment LLC office. It was nice, right in the middle of the business center. They sign in with security and security directs them both to Frank. Frank speaks with them briefly and escorts them to the fourth floor. "The office entrance is to your right. Mr. Jones is expecting you." Frank states.

"This is nice." Mitch pushes the glass door open. "You've been here before, right?"

"Yeah, a couple times, I was here when Jones had his grand opening of the office." Mike replies.

"Hi, we are here to see Mr. Jones. I'm Mitch."

"Yes. He is expecting you. He's finishing up his 10:00 then he will be right with you. Anything I can get for you? Water, tea, coffee, or soda?" asks the receptionist.

"I'll take an espresso?" says Mike.

The phone on the receptionist desk rings. She answers, "Hello Sir." She pauses, "Of course sir."

"Yes. We can get that for you. And actually, you both can follow me." Mitch and Mike follow behind the receptionist. "We are going to have you wait for Mr. Jones in here, he wanted to make sure you were comfortable, and our nap pod area is best."

"Thank you." says Mitch.

"No problem. You can stretch out if you like. And I'll bring your uh, espresso right away."

Mitch walks around. "Cool little gadgets. They got their name engraved everywhere, on everything, must have spent quite a bit on PR, pens, stress balls, key chains."

"Take whatever you like." Jones' voice interrupts.

"Mr. Jones?" Mitch stands.

"Yes." Jones responds.

"My name is Mitchell, but everyone calls me Mitch. It's nice to meet you Mr. Jones." Mitch extends out his hand. Mitch and Jones shake hands.

"Nice to meet you," Mr. Jones opens the button of his blazer before taking a seat.

"I'm glad we were able to schedule this meeting and you could come in Mitch. I've heard great things about you from Mike. Mike is the best and I trust his judgement. You know I'm only thirty-five. I wanted to start a company that will still be here and doing well in another thirty-five years. I see the longevity of Bitcoin investments and the potential to service people all over the world. Right now, we have investors and customers that exchange their Bitcoin for cash, all different types of currency, from all over the country, from Florida to Connecticut to Arkansas. One day we will have a significant customer basis in Africa."

"I appreciate that and everything you are trying to do. But what I really want to know is what is the risk?" Mitch asks.

"None, practically zero."

"There is always a risk." Mike follows up.

Jones looks at Mike. "When you keep growing and growing, like I do, and have yet to even come close to taking a loss on any deal, then there is practically no risk. Look at this place man. Bitcoin Investments paid for this, not me." Jones leans back, crossing his leg.

"When can an investor expect their investment back?" Mitch asks.

Jones answers. "I can promise you that I will get your money plus interest in less than a year."

Mitch questions Jones, "Less than a year?"

"Yes. You probably want to keep your money invested more than a year too. Once you see how much seven percent interest on 50,000 can get you. And as investment grows, that interest get you more and more." says Jones.

"How does it exactly work? Is there paperwork? A contract I can review?" Mitch asks Jones.

"Yes, take a look at this." Jones hands Mitch and Mike a portfolio book.

Mitch opens the portfolio. "We get a high interest return rate of what was it, seven percent?" Mitch continues. "That's it. What do you get? You must be getting something, or you wouldn't be doing this. No offense. I'm just saying we all have bills to pay."

"It's all in the portfolio. I get a fair share of your profits for my work in investing and managing the investment. I am just as vested in you making money, because that is the only way I make money. I make sure you make money," Jones states.

"What is your fair share?" Mitch asks.

"Two percent," states Jones.

"Two percent of money earned or two percent of the total portfolio?"

"Two percent of the money earned." Jones states.

"Is this the standard? Let me look this up on my phone."

"Generally, fees are per transaction on the portfolio, meaning for every trade and commission costs. But this is in the standard stock market not crypto market. It's easier and more beneficial to set a percentage. Because if you are doing a small or large trade transaction, the fee is the same. You end up paying more for a trade then the actual stock cost. This also ensures that my focus is on making you money rather than just making trades. Because I can make bad trades that you actually lose money on, but under the fee per transaction, I am still entitled to my fee for the trade," Jones states. "It's better for all parties involved."

"Okay." Mitch responds, "I am just curious, want to make sure I understand everything." Mitch is flipping through the portfolio.

"Not a problem at all. I get it. I think it's good to ask questions." Jones replies. "A cool thing we do over here at Bitcoin Investments is that we also donate to charities, NGOs and social justice initiatives. If you know an organization that we should consider in our grant funding annual review, please submit a recommendation.

"And we maintain full control over our investment?" Mike asks Jones.

"Yes, you can cash-out, sell, or trade as you like. Standard paperwork will be required, and it can take a few days to complete, but this standard. I am also here for you to give you advice on trades and selling, will give you my advice on what's best for you and what investments are optimal in the current market." Jones answers him.

"I don't know. I'm going to take this portfolio home with me. Maybe take some time to think it over." Mitch states.

"What is there to think about? You're young, no wife, no children, no responsibility. What are you really waiting for?

What are you scared of? Are you just going to keep working for someone else forever, while they get rich and make all the decisions? For what, why is someone else in control of your life, your destiny?" Jones doing his research on Mitch and Mike probably helped him too.

"I control my life. Yes, I work for someone else. But I enjoy my job, I have purpose. And you know, no disrespect or anything, I don't care what you may think about that." Mitch responds.

Jones quickly switches course. "You wouldn't be here if you were not interested. You can continue to do what gives you purpose and invest. That is the beauty of this. You don't need to worry. Let Bitcoin Investments worry about your future, that is what we are here for, and Bitcoin Investments is going to secure your future. You can continue to do the things that give your life purpose without worrying about when you are going to eat," Jones smiles.

"I told him you got him. We want to do this together. If we invest, it will be Mitch and I together, fifty/fifty and we will split the minimum investment amount of $5,000." Mike states.

"Listen, Mitch. I'm being straight with you. With others, usually I go through the whole mumble jumble and try to sell you on the innovation, how the new technology actually works. But you already know this. Mike tells me you mine or have interests in mining Bitcoin. So, you know this is real. You know how it works. Frankly I could use your expertise.

You would be an asset to Bitcoin Investments because of your knowledge. Perhaps even become a partner one day. That sounds good right?" Jones smiles at Mitch. "Bring in your own clients to invest too. This is the innovation on top of the innovation. We do this with U.S. dollars, why not Bitcoin. I'm sure others thought of this. But I was the first to do it. I am bold enough to take the risk and I'm so glad I did. This is the future and I want you to be a part of it."

"What do you say?" Mike pauses.

"Okay. Let's try it out. We can each invest $2,500 together and see how that goes. Maybe down the line, the next few months maybe we invest more. Never know, but currently and up to the foreseeable future, just that, nothing more." Mitch states.

"Alright!" Jones hits the table. "Let's make you some money." Jones gets up from the sofa and extends his hand. Mike and Jones shake hands.

"Feel free to relax, chill out here. There are drinks in the fridge. Remote control to the TV right there and the WIFI password is on the table too. My assistant has the paperwork for you to sign for the investment. Take your time, no rush, any questions let me know. My assistant will also arrange for how you will like to make the investment, cash, money order, Bitcoin, or whatever form is easiest for you both."

"Okay." Mitch says.

"Sounds good," Mike adds.

"We'll be in touch." Jones walks out. Mitch and Mike smile, thinking about the possibilities. Mitch and Mike stay and chat about the investment for some time, reading through the portfolio book. Mitch is asking Mike questions and Mike breezes through his questions. Mitch feels good about his meeting with Jones and conversations with Mike until Mike state's he doesn't have $1,250 to put down today.

"What do you mean you don't have the money?"

"I don't have it right now. I didn't expect to put down any money today. I thought we were just getting information and would discuss and perhaps come back later if we agreed." Mike states.

"I mean, I actually do have the money. Bitcoin, but technically it's tied up at the moment and I cannot physically access it, because I have to exchange my Bitcoin into cash, and I'm trying to get the most cash for my Bitcoin, so I have been waiting." Mike states.

"I don't know what you are waiting for. Either you want to do this or you don't." Mitch tells Mike. "You're the one that told me about this, brought me here and introduced me to Jones." Mitch states.

"Yes, I want to do this. I can pay my portion separately. I can come back and settle this all out. That is what we can do." Mike states.

Mitch is looking at the contract. He does not want to miss the opportunity. He is re-reviewing it to make sure that he will not be bound to pay or cover Mike's $1,250 if Mike doesn't pay it. The contract with Bitcoin Investments does not seem to make Mitch or Mike liable for each other's transactions and trades. It reads as if it is two separate contracts. Mitch goes to the receptionist, "Can I speak with Mr. Jones? I just have a couple of questions for him."

"He is in a meeting. Is there something I can help you with?" The receptionist asks.

"No. I would like to speak with him. It's about the investment contract. It will only take a few minutes, I can wait." Mitch states.

"I can have his contracts manager speak with you. Let me see if he is available," the receptionist states. She picks up the phone and pushes buttons, dialing the contract's manager's extension.

Mitch talks over the receptionist, "Oh no, that's okay. I would rather speak to Mr. Jones."

"The contracts manager is available. You can wait for him back in the conference room. He will be right with you." States the receptionist, she smiles.

Mitch walks back into the conference room. Mike is on the phone. He gets off the phone and asks, "How did it go? What did Jones say?"

"I didn't get to speak to him about making the contract separate." Mitch answers.

"It's just confusing since we are not in a formal partnership together. We don't have to be on the same contract. I'm sorry if we confused the company, but we are paying our money separately. I would like to pay today, and Mike will pay later." Mitch states.

"Okay. Not a problem. That was our mistake. Just give me some time to draw up the paperwork and new contract with just your name on it. Just give me some time to draft, edit, and submit to you for review," the contract manager states.

"Great!" Mitch responds. "I'll wait here."

"Mitch, I think I'm going to leave. I got all the information I need on the investment contract and I got places to be. I got to work on maximizing my Bitcoin for the most U.S. Dollar to get the $1,250 to invest too, so I got to get to it." states Mike.

"Okay. Yeah, get that done. The $1,250 is the priority right now. I understand." Mitch responds to Mike. Mike exits the conference room.

The contracts manager brings out the new investment contract. Mitch reviews it, takes him about twenty minutes. Mitch signs it and asks for a copy. After Mitch receives his copy, Mitch folds the document and places the document in an envelope. He takes the envelope and writes a check for $1,250, payable to: Bitcoin Investments.

On his way out of the building, Mitch runs into Frank downstairs, right outside of the leasing office. "I'm back." Mitch says to Frank. "I just want to say hello again and introduce us, because you are going to see a lot more of my face around here."

"I'll be here," Frank replies.

"Is he gone?" Jones asks.

"Yes." Frank answers.

"What happened in there?" Jones asks Mike.

"What do you mean? Everything went fine. He had a couple questions. Just nerves, nothing serious. He wrote us a check, right?! So, I would say everything went well." Mike responds.

"He is asking questions about contracts and percentage fees? How well do you know him? Who is he? Did you research him?" Jones asks.

"He is a gamer. He likes to take risks. He was already interested in cryptocurrency. I told him I knew some things. That impressed him and then he was hooked. I made him trust me." Mike states.

"But what does he do for a living?"

"He doesn't really talk about it. But he's just some chump that sits behind the desk punching a clock for the government." Mike states.

"He works for the government?! Why would you bring someone who works for the government here? That is too risky. We are trying to avoid government scrutiny!" Jones yells. "I can't believe you." Jones stammers. He is heated.

"My uncle works for the government; he basically is going to run the SEC one day. And I'm here." Mike states.

"That's different. You are not a liability because you are part of this. We are working together. Plus, we need you to get direct information. We don't know this man, we cannot be sure that we have not spooked him and that he's not going to the police right now," Jones states.

"I think you are over-thinking this. He was more worried about himself being held liable for my portion of the investment by you guys, by Mr. Jones and Bitcoin Investments. I should have brought a check. But I knew he could spot a fake check and frankly, I'm not too comfortable with giving my bank account information away." Mike responds.

"Oh, you don't trust us?" Jones asks. Frank and Jones laugh.

"I trust that we will do what we have to do to get this money." Mike responds.

"Next time, any more people need to be vetted through me first. You got it Mike?" Jones states.

"Yes." Mike answers Jones.

"Frank?" Jones questions Frank.

"I got it." Frank answers.

"Jones, I got this. Don't worry about me. Just do your fucking job and reel him back in for more. That's when we really get paid." Mike tells Jones.

"Okay, Frank any prospects?" Jones asks.

"A couple is coming in tomorrow and a middle-aged woman on Friday. She owns a hair and nail salon. The couple owns three fast food stores. They both got some money and seem like good credit, living in nice condos. I met them at that music festival about two weeks ago. We give them a good little taste of winning in the beginning and then we can get them to take out lines of credit, mortgage to invest with us. With these we are going to give them actual real money. I don't think paperwork is going to fly like with this Mitch guy because they are businesspeople. We give them a 25,000 return, money that we will get from Mitch. Then we get them to re-invest like 150,000 each. That's 300,000." Frank tells them.

"Okay. We got to stay on top of this though. We got to reel Mitch back in before we reel Frank's marks fully in. And this is just the beginning gentlemen. We got to keep it up, always looking for a new mark." Jones grins.

"We only got a few more days here before we move to a new location. Try to get anyone you have been working on in here by next Wednesday. Remember no family, no friends, no co-workers, or former co-workers either, it's too close. No one that knows you, new marks continue to work on them, but we will introduce them to Bitcoin Investments at the new location," Jones states.

* * *

Chris is reading the memo on Bitcoin from Mitch. He is learning a lot. Bitcoin is a digital currency, an electronically sourced unit of value that exists on the Internet and is not stored in a physical form. They are not issued by any government, but instead are generated and controlled through computer software operating on decentralized peer-to-peer networks. Users of digital currencies send units of value to and from addresses, which are unique strings of numbers and letters functioning like a public account number. Digital currency transactions are recorded on a publicly available, distributed shared ledger often referred to as a blockchain. Because digital currencies are transferred peer-to-peer, users can avoid traditional, regulated financial institutions and their fees, and presumably government regulation. "At least that is what they thought." Chris states out loud.

Chris knows that Bitcoin is setting the tone for the entire industry. And the industry will continue to evolve. Consumer protection is the key because it is now the money chasing the investor, not the investor chasing the money. "This is dangerous," says Chris, talking to himself. The entire crypto industry is regulated by unregulated white papers which present a significant information gap to miners, consumers, and investors. All the information the public is aware of is controlled by the company, and if the company is the one deciding how much information you should know or not know, the company is not revealing very much.

A common layout for cryptocurrency is the token platform. Under this layout, the company identifies the function of its company to create a particular platform that may provide goods or services. The company then shares information about a token that would be powered by a platform. The company then seeks funding for their idea for a specific platform and helps the launch of that platform. In exchange for the funding, individuals would receive tokens.

While they may be called tokens, it is not that simple. This specific token sale scheme to raise capital is like an initial public offering ("IPO") and is identified as initial coin offerings ("ICOs"). The idea is that an individual could get in on the ground floor of the launch of a token, and reap the reward were the token value to increase upon launch. ICOs can have two types of tokens: utility token and security token. Utility tokens are tokens offered for future use, access or service only on the application platform and are not subject to SEC regulation. However, the issuance of a token in exchange for an interest in the platform development is like obtaining a shareholder interest in stock. These are security tokens and are subject to SEC regulation.

The companies pushing the ICOs feed on the dream of the next Bitcoin to the tune of nearly $500 million lost by investors. Majority, as high as eighty-one percent, which were scams and never actually launched. The companies entice prospective investors with well-developed advertisements and polished marketing material. But when it came down to the details on the actual ICO, it was always the same messaging semantics and empty promises, no actual concrete substance on development and implementation. Common throughout ICOs is that there is no actual product to offer, let alone a product that had a tested and proven track record or metrics to evaluate potential growth and success. And the registration and disclosure requirements under securities law cannot fully address this problem. Current securities law does not take into consideration factors unique to digital assets like technology source code, blockchain governance, and how it is valued versus traditional reliance on financial statements.

These gaps in information consideration impact the disclosures made, usually through the ICO white papers. People must be informed on all of this to be able to make informed decisions to buy, use, or invest in cryptocurrency. These disclosures do not tend to be written in plain English. Potential investors must parse through extensive jargon and review of these papers can sometimes be difficult to understand for those without a technical or cryptography expertise.

Chris is reading this ICO white paper and he has more questions than answers. He calls in his anti-money laundering expert to have her review the white paper with him.

Chris hears a knock on his door. "Come in and please close the door."

"Good Afternoon," the expert says to Chris.

"I want to pick your brain about this ICO white paper I am reviewing. I just printed out another copy for you. You can take it from the printer right there." She waits for the printing to stop. Chris states, "Okay. That should be the last one." She takes the pages and sits in the chair. She moves her chair closer to the desk, so that she can have the paper on the table, where Chris can see what part of the white paper she is referring to and any notes she makes on the page. She begins to read and Chris resumes reading.

"I apologize. I want to give you some time to review. But I do have some questions." Chris states.

"Will the token give investors any rights or a portion of the project's earnings? Is there a cap on fundraising? And how does the project funding work? Are promoters issued tokens? If yes how many? And can they resell the tokens for profit?" Chris asks the expert.

She answers, "No rights to a portion of the ICO earnings and no cap on funding. It seems that funding of the project will be dedicated mainly to building the platform where the token will operate. There is also money dedicated to mainstreaming the token for wide usage and as a major digital currency." She sifts through the pages and folds the corner of some pages.

"And what about the number of tokens?" Chris asks.

"There is no set number of tokens that will be introduced in the universe for use on the platform. But there are two levels, or grades of tokens. There are no limits on the platform token. But there are limits on the non-platform token, with no more than five million tokens ever produced. The platform and non-platform tokens cannot be used interchangeably. You can buy either platform or non-platform-based tokens, where the cost of the non-platform-based token is higher than platform based tokens." She said.

"And I still don't know exactly who is running the ICO? Do you know? Have you seen it in there?" Chris asks her.

She responds, "No." The expert is turning pages and highlighting. "I don't see that, just Bitcoin Investments is identified as one investor, which is interesting, and not necessarily in a good way. I also notice that the white paper is extremely vague on how the ICO keeps investors' money secure. You cannot directly purchase the token; you have to send Bitcoin to a receiving email address given by the ICOs promoters and then the investor will receive a transfer of the token to the same email address they used for delivery of Bitcoin."

Chris nods. "I want you to keep your eye on this ICO and Bitcoin Investments. Might just be a fake name being used. Monitor any updates and actions in the media. All public information should be collected and cataloged. I am then going to have you…"

"If I may, um, is this ICO under investigation?" She asks. "I only ask because I know the IRS is looking at some platform called Eclipse that does cryptocurrency exchanges to real money, like the U.S. dollar."

"Not yet. They have not opened their ICO yet for investment and this white paper is identified as tentative and subject to edits. But I imagine it will largely stay the same." Chris answers.

"I am happy to do so." She closes the door behind her.

Ultimately, extending the securities regulatory regime to digital assets and cryptocurrencies may not work, and disclosure requirements are not an adequate remedy to address ICO concerns. Despite this, ICOs have raised billions, rivaling traditional sources of capital funding.

CHAPTER 7

TURF WAR

———

Commodity or security? Well what day is it? Perhaps it is a security on Wednesday but sixty days later, it could be a commodity. So, who has jurisdiction? The Security Exchange Commission or the Commodity Futures Trading Commission? They are not mutually exclusive. CFTC's jurisdiction lies with fraud and market manipulation in interstate commerce. SEC's jurisdiction lies with the offer and sale of securities. A crypto instrument could be both a commodity and a security. Both agencies were really trying to stay neutral in enforcement actions. The agencies look to the actual substance and purpose of the crypto activity in question to decide when and how to apply agency regulations.

Virtual currency or token classified as a commodity subject to CFTC regulation is most commonly found where derivative contract, meaning retaining utility value in future use of the token. An instrument is classified as a security subject to SEC regulation when rights attached are typical rights of a security including ownership and entitlement to future profits or value in the enterprise. A virtual instrument is most commonly found where tokens are essentially sold through the funding mode or an investment contract.

An initial coin offering ("ICO") is not automatically a security, because at the basic level it tokens are issued through the ICO and tokens are not securities. It is the way the token is sold and the reasonable expectation of purchasers that determines if the token is a security or not. You can usually distinguish an instrument that is a commodity from a security by looking to the benefits and/or rights attached to the instrument upon investment or purchase.

And did it even matter? Somehow and either way, with more than one government agency in the fight, someone was going to lose, and it was not going to be the government.

"Can you pull up the latest financial tech, and stock market news updates for me?" Moto asked his assistant. He began his regular morning routine of catching up on the latest updates to the market, one line grabbed by attention. In bold letters printed: SEC Press Announcement: Opening of Inquiry into Eclipse.

"Shit! I have to get the Board on the phone!"

Moto calls his assistant. "Susan! Schedule a meeting with the Board within the next twenty-four hours!" Moto resumes reading the press announcement.

Eclipse is a virtual currency exchange platform. Customers can use the platform to exchange their Bitcoin for other virtual currency and fiat currency. Eclipse also serves as a wallet, storing virtual currency on short term and long-term periods. They had been operating basically unregulated, and they were celebrating in the success.

The board meeting is scheduled. Rather than meet at the company headquarters, the meeting was at the Gallagher Firm. "Please drop your phones in this basket on the way in. No electronics are allowed. This is a highly sensitive conversation. For those who are unable to attend in person, they can schedule another in-person meeting with the firm. No teleconference option will be made available." The firm lead assistant repeated as people entered the board meeting room.

Brad looking around states to himself, "BC Trusts lawyered up, big time." This is an understatement as the legal team grew from just Brad to a firm of over one-hundred attorneys and dozens of legal support staff. BC Trusts went out and hired an entire firm to complete an investigation, assessment of their business practices, and whether the SEC or CFTC compliance rules applied. BC Trusts still retained a significant stake in Eclipse. And any investigation would impact the value of Bitcoin, as Moto was a partner, and he held significant ownership of Bitcoins more than the average owner at least.

The firm lead counsel begins to speak, "On behalf of the Gallagher Firm, I would like to thank you for trusting our firm with your legal needs. We are here for you morning, noon, or night. I don't want to bore you with a review of the technical stuff. I think you know more all about how the Eclipse system works and its functions with Bitcoin. It is a good thing you came to us, because your concerns about potential impact and backlash as major investors holding a large stake in Eclipse is valid." The round conference table is made of cherry wood. In the center, stands the lead counsel with four other attorneys, two on each side. Fitting about 50 people around the table and the mics hanging from the ceiling above chairs to ensure all persons at the table can hear each other when speaking. Brad grabs a water and pastry from the coffee bar.

Sam follows up, "From what we have been advised by our in-house counsel, Brad, everything hedges on the Howey test. What is your legal advice on how the Howey test will apply to Eclipse?"

"I'm glad you raised Howey. That is where we were heading." The firm lead counsel continues speaking. "I would say it's refreshing to have a client that is knowledgeable about the business and legal implications. This helps with litigation."

"Wait, you expect litigation? These things do not go to court. There will be a settlement offer?" Sean interjects.

"The firm stands behind the decision you all make. It doesn't have to be today. But we do have to come to an agreement on how we move forward and the sooner, the better for legal strategy. The firm does recommend that we take this all the way to court. The government is setting policy standards based on settlement agreements that cannot be reviewed by a court. Essentially the government is punishing persons for activity that is not clearly illegal, and so far, the government is not being required, nor challenged to prove illegality."

"I don't think we should let this drag out. A settlement offer should be fully considered as an option." responds Sean.

Sam coughs and looks at Moto.

Moto states, "I don't think this is the place for the Board to discuss this and we should discuss and come back to the firm. Our purpose today is to understand the risks and get advice on the legal status of Eclipse. If we can get back to how Howey applies?"

Sean folds his arms across his chest. The lead counsel begins to answer Moto, "The Howey test provides that an instrument is a security where there is an investment of money in a common enterprise with a reasonable expectation of profits from other entrepreneurial or managerial efforts. A token sale can be offering a security, if buyers expect the token to increase in value based on the issuer's efforts or retain some financial interest in the enterprise. Unfortunately, Howey is retroactive and applies all the way back. Even though none of us knew Howey applied to virtual currencies or assets until recently. If your account holders are expecting to earn a profit by putting their Bitcoin in your trust or their Bitcoin to increase in value while in your trust, then we could be in SEC territory. Similarly, if you guys put your Bitcoins in

Eclipse with the intent or expectation to make an investment or receive an interest when the development of the Eclipse platform was complete, then we are in SEC territory."

The attorney to the left of lead counsel states, "We will need your cooperation in this process. We will request documents, emails, among other communications with or about Eclipse to assess the intent of BC Trust's decision to have Eclipse hold or store its Bitcoin."

The lead counsel resumes, "Today, we will like to conduct brief interviews with each of you one on one, if that's okay." She looks around the room. Everyone seems to nod in agreement except Sam and Moto.

"Look, I'm a silent partner in BC Trusts. I'm not in charge of the day to day operations of BC Trusts. I'm not making any decisions, I'm just here in an advisory capacity and I didn't advise on this Eclipse venture. I got nothing to do with this so I'm leaving," Moto states.

"The government and the law may not share your position that the title silent partner absolves you of liability or legal requirements. It is best at this time, that everyone cooperates with us and that we are all on the same page moving forward." Lead counsel states.

Moto gets up and leaves.

"I have to attend to some family obligations at home. But I can reschedule for later this week," states Sam.

"Okay. Make sure to speak with the receptionist on the way out to schedule that appointment." Lead counsel smiles.

"I can't make any commitments at this time. My family comes first." Sam states.

"I'm sure we can find something. We can work around your schedule." Lead counsel responds.

"I don't know," Sam states and leaves the conference room.

The lead counsel proceeds with speaking to those remaining in the room, Sean and Brad.

"The SEC and CFTC are of course players here. But there is another and they have been awfully quiet. And this is concerning. FinCen." Lead counsel continues. "The Financial Crimes Enforcement Network, under the U.S. Department of Treasury, if you have not heard of them, you better get familiar with them and quick." Her assistants drop a bound packet in front of each of them. "FinCen enforces the Bank Secrecy Act, anti-money laundering rules. If you guys were just regular Bitcoin users engaging in transactions, there would be nothing to worry about. But we are here because you are not average. And more likely than not you are subject to their regulation as an 'exchanger.' Why, because you have accepted Bitcoin from persons and transmitted that Bitcoin in another transfer, sale, purchase, or exchange through BC Trusts. Not to worry, the packet in front of you contains a breakdown of classification and applicability of laws under FinCen, the CFTC, SEC, and the IRS." Lead counsel explains.

Brad states, "And as an exchanger, we are considered money transmitters. We were supposed to register with Fin-Cen as a money services business."

The lead counsel clasps her hands in front of her suit. "At this time, we are going to get started with the individual interviews, so that we give you our best assessment on liability and strategy going forward. I expect this to take some time, so feel free to get some coffee and use the bathroom if you like. Please meet me at the receptionist desk when you are ready."

* * *

Sam gets up and exits the board room. He steps down the glass and steel staircase, where he sees the reception desk. He walks past it. "Mr. Boone?!", the receptionist calls out. She gets up and steps from behind the desk, "Mr. Sam Boone?!" The receptionist voice begins to trail, as Sam continues to the elevator. He heads down in the elevator to the office building lobby, out the revolving door.

Sam is never home this early. He had time to go through his mail. Sam did not check his mail too often, maybe once a week or once every two weeks. He never got a lot of mail, because Sam had set up automatic payment through his bank for most of his bills and recurring expenses. He kept a detailed account and when he forgot to check the mail, the cleaner he hired to come to his house once a month would put the mail on the dining room table. Sam saw the mail on his table and after that board meeting, he could use the distraction. Sam shifts through the mail. Mostly envelopes, some magazines, and the rest junk mail. Pulling the letter opener out of the desk drawer, Sam opens some of the envelopes. Sam then comes to a legal manila envelope; the sender is the Internal Revenue Service and return service is requested. He opens the envelope quickly and pulls out the papers. Sam reads the papers, *Warning Letter that Federal Tax Laws May Have Been Violated*.

The IRS was threatening him for allegedly not reporting income he earned from selling some of his Bitcoin. He keeps reading the letter over and over. A lot of citation to legal codes, but no confirmation of actually how much income he earned and how much taxes he actually owed. Matter of fact, there is no confirmation anywhere in the letter that the IRS knew if he made a profit on Bitcoin or not. "How did they even know I own Bitcoin? How did they get this information?" Sam stares at the letter. He thinks this could be linked to the Eclipse investigation. He opens his Tor browser and plugs in "Eclipse" and "SEC investigation" into the search box. Some things popped up in the browser search, but there is nothing new that was not discussed earlier, and the private investigator and their lawyer, Brad, was bound to find out more. But he didn't want to burden them with his issue.

He walked to his home office. Sam opens his cabinet file and quickly places the IRS letter in an obscure folder. His wife would be home soon, and he did not want to add to her worry. He pulls out his tax filing to review later and locks the cabinet. His income is taxed at twenty-four percent, and he will remain in that bracket even with any income earned from Bitcoin. Sam is thinking. Trying to estimate any profit he made from an exchange or sale. "It couldn't have been no more than $100,000 if any." He sits back down at his desk and grabs a pen and paper. Tapping the pen, he begins with January. He couldn't remember exact amounts and didn't have any expectation that he would need to keep track of it. He looks down at his paper: January: $3,000, February: $0. "Yes, none in February or March, I was on vacation." He states out loud. "April, I don't know. May I don't know, June and July, I think maybe five or six thousand, no nothing more than a thousand." And he writes it down.

"Hello sweetie." His wife says. "This is a nice surprise! You're never home from work this early."

He responds, "You just getting in, I didn't hear you."

"You know how you are when you're in this office." She kisses him on the cheek. "What's going on with the SEC investigation?"

"We met with the firm today and discussed some options. This is just the first meeting, so still early stages but there is some hope." He responds.

"What did they say about the level of exposure you would have personally; can you be held liable and have to pay out of bank accounts or assets?" His wife asks.

"We didn't get to that. But I am going to ask."

"Okay, please make sure you do. I asked you yesterday to talk to them about it today."

"I know. I will. I promise." He answered.

His wife peering over his shoulder says, "You're working on a list?"

"Oh this, just some work stuff," He turns the paper over.

Looking at the paper, she asks him, "everything okay?"

"Yea. Nothing to worry about. Babe, do you know if we sold any Bitcoin last year."

"I remember once or twice. But could be more, I don't know." She says.

"I think my memory is going." He manages to laugh. And she smiles at him. "I told you."

Sam tells his wife, "I'm finishing up somethings in here, and I'll be right out for dinner."

"Okay." His wife closes the door behind herself.

Turning back over the paper, he cannot remember anymore. He's just not sure and will be guessing. Not helpful either. Sam put the paper down and goes back to his computer. He logs into some of the cryptocurrency messaging boards. And everybody is talking about the IRS.

One user wrote, "It is Eclipse." Another user replied, "What is the point of an anonymous network, if they going to just report everything." A reply to that said, "Clearly it was anonymous between only users, but they were tracking our transactions individually." Scrolling down to read more of the messages on the message board subject chain Sam reads, "What happened to our right to be forgotten?" Blockchain activity uses blockchain technology that should be encrypted to protect the right to be forgotten.

People are pointing to Eclipse as the culprit. Eclipse is under investigation, and it's no secret that the SEC probably handed over information they got from Eclipse to the IRS. And while the press release on the investigation was just issued, the length and extent of what the SEC had already done was unknown. Sam reads on the message board, "We cannot use them anymore, pulling out now." Sam assumes they are referring to Eclipse and continues to read the responses on the message board. "I do not think there is an explicit requirement that any Bitcoin sales be reported to a government agency by third parties," Sam nods his head in agreement. He thinks to himself, what the hell were the execs at Eclipse doing?

But Eclipse's focus of concern is saving its own skin. As of matter of practice, the SEC is more lenient on those who cooperate with the SEC. Eclipse will be subject to fines, but they were taking their chances at getting a no prosecution deal that imposed a smaller fine for cooperation. This will steer them clear of any penalties that will restrict their leadership from participating in the trade and securities market in the future.

Sam understands Eclipse trying to save themselves, but why didn't they come to Moto and I first? We may have been able to help them. Now they are screwing everyone over and if people are pulling out of Eclipse, BC Trusts will have to pull out too or risk losing it all. But it will be suspicious for them to pull everything out of Eclipse with the ongoing SEC investigation. Sam will talk to Moto and suggest pulling out some Bitcoin from Eclipse, around twenty-five percent.

Sam is not the only one who receives an IRS letter today, so does Mike. He is in shock. He followed the rules like his uncle Chris instructed him. If he is not selling Bitcoin or seeking investment, he does not have to register with the SEC. But Mike is making a profit, earning income and property according to the IRS. He thought miners like him are protected. How could the government do this and why didn't his uncle tell him? He is supposed to know these things.

Thoughts are running through Mike's mind. He has never been in trouble, at least not serious trouble like this. He can't have the government coming after him. "How am I going to get the money to pay the government?" Mike says out loud. Mike responds the only way he knows how, mining more and more Bitcoin. "I can mine Bitcoin and exchange Bitcoin for USD to pay them. I will owe the IRS again next year. But I will have money from Jones soon and I will pay everything, so no fines, interest fees, or issues." He says to himself. It is the only way he can make money and make it quickly.

Mike is not alone in his panic. Mike and Sam, along with 10,000 other Bitcoin owners received warning letters from the IRS, reflective of a strategic and resource intensive effort. The IRS is taking advantage because the rules are not clear. The fight for jurisdiction by the agencies continues to take different forms.

Joe is done playing catch up. He feels that the CFTC must be more proactive in its approach, not just waiting for a violation to occur.

Joe pulls his boss aside, "we need to take a page out of the SEC handbook. I do not know if this is within the CFTC's authority, but we can ask legal for their opinion on that later. What about CFTC getting the tech community involved? They can build us a tool that allows us to collect data across major blockchains."

"But the industry is pretty dicey as it is about government involvement in this area." His boss responds.

"Remember this is not about crushing innovation but about protecting investors from fraud and manipulation. We can issue a preliminary solicitation notice to get a feel for how the public and industry will react. If not good, we can scrap it and right it off as preliminary information to gather better understanding on what can or cannot be done, and the consequences. Simply, market research, if it is good, then we can tout it as support for the agency and data tool." Joe replies.

"Okay, I'll bite. Describe to me how this will look and what is the specific request from the tech companies? It's a small community. They know each other, and in their business, they have to work with the individuals and companies that we have concerns with on risk and compliance. And now you are going to ask them to help us monitor them, and their former colleagues, friends, and neighbors, the optics do not look good," Joe's boss states.

"I do not think anyone is against CFTC doing their job because this community is also made up of investors. They just want that law and regulation to be clear. We are running around in circles and chasing one bad actor at a time as we find out. With a data tool we may be able to finally assess on a larger scale, beyond just one actor." Joe responds.

Joe's boss gives him permission to push ahead and draft a proposal.

"Let me be clear, you can explore this proposal nothing more. It may be beneficial to have your ideas developed on paper. This does not mean that the agency will actually move forward with it," the boss states.

Joe replies, "Yes, of course."

"And do not discuss this with anyone outside of me. No one else should be privy to this information at this time," The boss states.

"Of course," Joe responds and heads back to his desk. He begins to put his thoughts down. Not in any particular order but wants to have a rough draft as soon as possible. Joe has his boss's attention on this for now, but that can easily change. A change in agency priorities has made CFTC investigators work obsolete before and more times than he could count. This is the nature of the system. Joe will do what is asked of him and he believes that cryptocurrency should be the CFTC's top priority.

In theory, they will need all size businesses and tech firms on board. They will need their expertise to build a tool that provides data for the most widely used blockchain ledgers based on transaction volume. The tool should be able to pull data from the universe of available information in an easily reviewable format. To help ensure data completeness and accuracy, there will be articulated standards, processes, and procedures that govern how information is extracted and converted. As well as any other tools that may be used to manipulate and/or transform the data for other use purposes. He would need to figure out what firms have the technical capacity to do this. As the solicitation notice can be written in a way that is geared toward those firms' business model or released at an industry-government roundtable held in that firms' largest client area. They would probably also be able to target the right firms with an appearance from CFTC leadership that encourages submission of proposals to the solicitation notice at the financial tech conferences usually held in California and Washington D.C.

It is the end of the business day and Joe left the office to go to a nearby pub about a block away. Its happy hour and he is meeting up with his old college friend, Brad, for some advice.

Brad and Joe are taking shots at the bar. They are waiting on their hot wings to come out. They are catching up. A lot had changed since college and they had not got a chance to really hang out since college. Joe went out east to New

York to complete graduate school and ended up staying in New York for work. That is when he started working for the government. He started out at the Department of Treasury but moved to CFTC within a few years. About a year ago, Joe moved back out to California with an office transfer request and promotion.

"You're back, for good?" Brad asks Joe.

"I missed home; you know. I missed the trees and the beach, just the basics." Joe tells Brad.

"Oh, that's what you told the Feds, and they bought it." Brad chuckles. "I expect more of them for my tax dollars." Brad states.

"Your tax dollars are paying for these drinks and wings too." Joe chuckles.

"Don't remind me, but it's the least you can do." Brad grins.

"But you know I can't complain. I got a great career, I love my job, and the work I do. My colleague is, uhh, so so, but what can you do? Nothing is perfect," Joe responds.

"But most of your family is out east too? They moved right after you did." Brad asks Joe.

"Yeah, part of the reason why I stayed in New York for so long too. I got comfortable with my position. I needed a challenge." Joe responds.

"But now is the time to grow, take a chance and go where my career leads me. I got a promotion with the CFTC that's how I got here, so I will be here for a little while, at least a few years." Joe states to Brad.

"That's great man, I am proud of you man." Brad states.

"Yeah thanks. I surprised myself by the little things I missed from home. Like Dave's. You know if Dave's is still open?" Joe asked.

"Daves?" Brad asks.

"The pub with the arcade downstairs, used to have five-dollar drafts and ladies' night on Fridays." Joe states.

"I don't think so. A lot of places went out of business. People sought to cash in. Sold their property to commercial real estate companies and luxury residential development firms and blocks were taken down one at a time."

"Gentrification," Joe states and drinks his beer.

"I stopped by the barbershop. You know the one we use to go to off Linden. Nothing looks the same. The whole neighborhood done changed. The community is gone." Joe takes a gulp of his beer.

"What is going on with you?" Joe asks Brad.

"You know out here being a lawyer." Brad states. "I actually make more money just consulting and advising without all the work." Brad continues. "I do a lot of corporate work, securities, and stocks and trades." Brad takes sip of his drink.

"You know you should think about going private. A lot of money out here to go around and I know the government don't pay much, I imagine you still paying loans."

"I'll be okay. Loans wiped clean after ten years. One of the perks, working for the government," Joe tells him.

"Besides, a lot of nefarious actors out there and I work for the government, no one would hire me."

"You will be surprised. All you have to do is talk a good game and talk as if you can capitalize on your contacts and access. They will pay you just because of that. Your title and experience will get you in the door, because they want to know how government agencies think and operate for investigations and when enforcing regulations. That is an asset for them. Because they have essentially a heads up and can exploit procedure to their benefit if they are subject to a regulation or investigation. You will know what to do, what is going to happen, and thus how to advise them." Brad tells Joe.

"I actually wanted to pick your brain, Brad, about on something." Joe says.

"Okay, shoot." Brad responds.

"I wanted to ask you about cryptocurrency." Joe replies. Brad puts his chicken wing down.

"Cryptocurrency, everybody wants to talk about crypto!" Brad states. "You are not the first person to ask me. I usually charge people by the hour for advice. But for you, I'll give you the family discount." Brad chuckles.

"Well only if that family discount is free." Joe states.

"Yeah yeah. Of course! What do you want to know?" Brad asks.

"Well I think I understand how it works. What I am curious about is, how does one record transactions on the blockchain? For potential use to determine or understand behaviors through data driven tools?" Joe asks.

"I don't think that is possible. I mean that is the whole purpose behind the design of blockchain technology. Even if data is pulled, that data is no longer relevant the minute after it is pulled, because the blockchain keeps building more blocks on top of itself with each transaction. The data is different all the time, continuously changing every minute." Brad explains.

"Well what if I just want to keep pulling the data continuously, and then be able to pick and choose what I want later based on set factors for filtration?" Joe asks.

"Theoretically you can pull all the data you want to your hearts content. But you're not really getting anything you can filter. It's just numbers. You can't identify anything or anyone." Brad responds.

"What about the public keys though? I know it's not complete identification of the user, but it's a way to filter out to see transactions."

"Okay so you see the transactions. And then what do you do? You still can't identify the person. What are you going to say, public key 347 engaged in this? So!"

"Well who said I want to identify who the person is?" Joe asks.

Brad looks away from Joe and stares straight ahead while he drinks the last of his beer, "You do work for the CFTC."

"Oh, you thought I didn't know." Brad looks at Joe in his eyes. "Look is there something specific you are trying to get, and I can tell you if it's possible or not. But the way you have framed it so far, the answer is no. If not, I got things to do." Brad states, pulling $100 out of his wallet. "Check please!" Brad states to the bartender.

"I want to know how data from major blockchain based tokens or coins can be pulled based on transaction volume segregated by public key into an easily reviewable format in real-time," Joe asks.

"Okay I can get back to you on that, okay." Brad states. "Great to see you buddy! Drinks and food are on me!" Brad leaves Joe at the bar.

CHAPTER 8

THE GOOD, THE BAD, AND THE UGLY

———

The people are chugging along to power the platform and improving the protocol, stuck in front of computer screens, addicted to the hope of imminent money as fast food bags and soda bottles littered around them in their closet-like space. From sunup to sundown, miners keep chugging and keep the platform running, celebrating the end of crypto winter and beginning of crypto spring.

The people are optimistic with Bitcoin's value rocketing to $12,000. The institutionalization of crypto is helping. Payment in bitcoin is now commonplace in online shopping. Retailers and some restaurants even allow customers to pay in Bitcoin. Accessibility is key, where people can purchase and cash out Bitcoin at ATMs. It is everywhere, the young, middle-aged, working class, and wealthy all knew about Bitcoin. And gave renewed attention to developing and underdeveloped nations that wanted to ensure all its citizens, including the un-banked population would benefit from the global economy.

Mitch is home. It's Sunday afternoon and he is laying on his couch reading up on the crypto stock market. This is what he has done all weekend. He would not call himself an expert, but he was crypto savvy now. He committed himself to learning everything he could since Mike and his investment with Bitcoin Investments about three months ago. He is a subscriber to all the financial tech magazines and journals now. He gets regular alerts and news updates on everything crypto. It was helpful because at work most of his caseload under the new chairman, his old department supervisor, Chris, is focused on cryptocurrency on the dark web with the Locke Market case and Eclipse, BC Trusts inquiry. His work was all about looking into the crypto-market trusts and exchanges.

The crypto stock market is booming with the rise in the value of Bitcoin. Everyone is talking about crypto all over the news, even news coverage by non-tech and financial media. People are excited and hopeful for the future. New crypto and blockchain businesses are created every day. Mitch is glad he got in before the boom and now he is seeing his stock value rise. Mitch wants to cash in even more and Mitch thinks he can make a couple of trades from his portfolio to make even more money. He calls Jones.

"Hey Jones, it's me Mitch. How is it going?"

"Good, got a client meeting in a few. But what can I do for you?" Jones replies.

"I want to trade some of my current stock for a few shares in Creed and Manna each." Mitch states.

"I don't think it's a good time to work with those companies you mentioned, Creed and Manna. They are young companies and no one I know has ever worked with them. No stability there, too much risk." Jones responds.

"I know this is your area of expertise, but I have done a lot of research and Creed and Manna are a good bet. The market is in a good place, Manna and Creed stock prices are rising every day. I have been reading the market price analyses and crypto news. Even studying the crypto stock charts. I think even a short-term trade will be beneficial." Mitch states.

"You know though, I know about some great options for you too. I can put together some options on paper and give it you. I wouldn't be doing my job if I let you just trade away your investment without considering all your options. And I have worked with these companies before. But if you want, it is your money I can give you a check for half of what your investment has grown. That is 30K," Jones states.

"300K?! My investment has grown to 60K already?!" Mitch interrupts Jones.

"Yes! Like you said the market is booming. You turned your half of the initial investment, 1,250 into 60K." Jones responds.

"That is way more than the 7% interest! I'm not complaining I'm just excited! I'm going to buy a house!" Mitch responds.

"That's the market. Never know what to expect. I'm about to walk into my client meeting. He is having a great day like you too. I'm going to show him some investment options. I can give you a call and discuss some of these lucrative investments with you too." Jones tells Mitch.

"That's great to hear! We'll speak soon then!" Mitch hangs up the phone.

He logs into his client profile on the Bitcoin Investments portal. The portal is where he can see the growth and value of his investment. Monthly financial investment statements are also issued and available on the portal for Mitch to see any and all trades, cryptocurrency fluctuations in value, and net loss and growth.

Mitch sees an incremental steady increase for the last few months averaging between three to four percent. His current investment value is at 30,000. "30,000!" Mitch states out loud. "This must be a mistake. This is nowhere near 60,000!"

Mitch calls Jones but his call goes straight to voicemail. He leaves a message, "Mr. Jones this is Mitch I need you to give me a call right away. My portfolio account on the website does not show my investment value at 60,000 like you said." Mitch remembers that Jones said he was meeting a client. "That's why he didn't answer my call." Mitch says to himself. Mitch is frustrated.

Jones does not call Mitch back that day. Instead, Mitch receives an email from Jones that states the network system is down and this is impacting updates to the Bitcoin Investments portal. Jones did include two attachments in the email. One email attachment looked like a scanned copy of Mitch's portfolio investment reflecting a surge increase in the last three weeks of his investment to 30,000. But was Mitch and Mike's investment together that totaled 60,000, not Mitch's individual investment. Maybe he heard Jones wrong, he did cut him off. He was just so excited he probably did not hear him all the way. And the $60,000 in total made sense because Bitcoin has increased in value by over 1,000%. Four hundred percent on $2,500 adds up to $10,000.

The second attachment in the email is a list of some crypto stocks Jones recommends for Mitch to invest in. Mitch writes an email response back to Jones asking Jones,

"Please investigate Creed and Manna because I want to invest. I know we talked about it earlier and I understand where you are coming from on risk, but I can lessen the risk to my portfolio by investing separately into Creed and Manna. I will not sell or trade my current portfolio I have with you. I want to keep that. Please let me know how can move forward on Creed and Manna. I'll look at your recommendations too. Give me a call as soon as possible. Thanks."

Creed is transforming the legal field by changing how entities create, use, and enforce contracts. By leveraging blockchain technology, smart contracts are self-managed along with the business' contract relationships, practices, and automated processes. Smart contracts are enabling people to create their own tokens. Something they could not have imagined, the production of digital currencies on a mass scale. The potential of non-traditional investors and non-institutional stakeholders to garner funding and investment through smart contracts is amazing. Smart contracts can be used for raising funding in the form of cryptocurrency through pre-sale of a product. The sale of virtual shares in a crypto stock-based entity has also worked. Perhaps even the auction of goods could work. It is a reality now that autonomous organizations can have multiple funding streams, thereby supporting speech and ideas. Perhaps the principles had lived through innovation.

Creed is also trying to develop the technological infrastructure to support an infinite number of transactions to be processed per second. This technology is called sharding. As part of this technology development, the Creed platform seeks to increase capacity to validate transactions—proof of stake—by moving from 1 Creed network to 100 networks within a single validator pool. As more computing power is added in the form of new shards, the network will be able to increase the number of transactions and move to endless proof of stake capacity to ensure scalability. Ultimately, the validation of transactions is set to take less energy and predicted to be powered by device weaker than computers like a smartphone.

The crypto Manna platform serves as a method of payment and currency exchange online using the distributed ledger. The ultimate benefit from using the crypto Manna platform is that users can exchange money in the currency they desire and facilitate payments without the inherent risk of loss of value due to market fluctuations, and fees during the exchange. You could use anything, the Euro, USD, even Bitcoin on crypto Manna. The platform eliminates the extra steps and inconvenience of exchanging USD to crypto. Everything is literally one hop away. You save time and increase global commerce. People take for granted the ability to make international calls instantly, but that was not always the case. Crypto Manna is betting on this same goal for global commerce of crypto. The plan is to be able to confirm payments in only five to ten seconds and access to anyone with internet.

Now, crypto Manna and Creed are like Bitcoin in its use of blockchain technology but still different, part of the natural progression of technology and innovation. By the nature of the market was not changing the supply itself, but the type of supply offered to the market. The market will decide what to do next. With cryptocurrency and the blockchain technology development being pushed by Creed and crypto Manna, Bitcoin is ensured to have a steady and increasing consumer base. Increase in access and convenience would bring BC Trusts more consumers and more transactions. People may not know what they want right now, but when they see what the market can offer, they will need it. And they will continue to need it because they can use and access it right from their fingertips. The internet has made book companies into global market monopolies. The internet makes the possibilities for digital currency endless.

Mitch and Jones speak about investments, calls and emails go back and forth over the next two weeks.

"I recommend that you invest at a minimum at least $50,000 in the stocks if you are going to do it all." Jones tells Mitch.

"Really, that's a lot, seems a stark increase, very high, from my last investment." Mitch states.

"You see that the crypto market is booming and the value of crypto is increasing every day. You can get shares at the lowest price you are going to get now or wish you had when the value continues to increase and thus the price of shares increases too." Jones tells Mitch.

Mitch responds, "I know but I have no way of getting that …"

Jones talks over Mitch, "you got to spend money to make money. You know that and it's been proven. That's why we have made money together. With $50,000 Mitch, this way, you can see real return on your investment. I'm talking six-digit numbers Mitch."

"The crypto market is doing good, especially for Creed and Crypto Manna." Mitch states.

"Bitcoin Investments does not have to invest it all for you at once. We can break the stock buys up by quarter. Buy a few now and test the market. Keep the rest in a trust earning interest, we can diversify your portfolio. Trust me. We do this all the time with other clients. We can offer this to you too." Jones suggests to Mitch.

"I'll see what I can do. I'll give you a call back." Mitch responds.

"Okay. Sounds good, let me know what you want to do, either way." Jones replies.

Mitch decides that the quickest way for him to secure $50,000 to invest is through a home loan. He has some student loan debt, but he has been making consistent payments for the last seven years, and the debt will be forgiven in ten years. He hopes that by showing he always pays his monthly bill and the few years left on his debt, he can ease any flags for his home ownership mortgage application at the bank. Mitch applies for a home loan and is approved for $150,000. At a high interest rate of 8%, but Mitch is not worried. He tells himself that he will pay it off in no time by next quarter. In three months, Mitch is supposed to receive a check from Jones on his investment returns from Bitcoin Investments.

Mitch looks at homes in San Francisco. Mitch is working with his real estate agent, Shelly, to focus on homes that are fixer-uppers but have some character. Or as his real-estate agent Shelly says, "Strong bones." Mitch laughs every time she says it. He is primarily viewing homes near public transportation. Access is important to him. Mitch figured if he can get a home for $100,000 or less then he would be able to invest the remaining $50,000 in crypto stock. Shelly explained to him that meant he would have to open his geographic area and go a little further outside of San Francisco, and he couldn't get a house, maybe a duplex or a condo, but not a house.

Mitch settles for a condo, the listing price is $110,000 but Shelly can negotiate the seller down to $100,000. There are added closing costs and fees, but Mitch just dips into his savings for that. Things would be tight for the next six months, but it would be worth it. Two weeks after living in his new condo, Mitch goes to the bank and transfers the remaining $50,000 to his personal checking account. Mitch gets a certified check issued by his bank payable to Bitcoin Investments. Mitch gives Jones the $50,000 check to buy stocks in Creed and Crypto Manna. Mitch is excited and so is Jones.

* * *

It is now more than a fad. Virtual money, cryptocurrency, whatever you call it, it's here to stay. Bitcoin made its mark, forcing existing payment systems to reevaluate their payment systems. The people are demanding better services, and not going to be pushed around anymore. Banks are even exploring the adoption of cryptocurrencies. No one can deny that virtual money provides numerous advantages in terms of security, transferability, transparency, and inflation resistance. A potentially faster, fairer financial system should garner mass support and appeal.

Everything was going well, but the SEC had a different agenda. The SEC is steering resources toward the division's Cyber Unit to tackle cyber-related threats and misconduct. Crypto is increasingly taking up a buckle of this, with over 225 ongoing investigations. The investigation numbers are reflective of the increase in suspicious activity reports involving cryptocurrency to FinCen.

U.S. lawmakers are focusing on the misuses of crypto, as if the potential for criminal exploitation of it is a problem unique to digital money, although it could exasperate it. It's really an excuse to hold on to power, as the U.S. dollar is not merely money used in the United States but throughout the world and serves as the standard for the valuation of most currencies throughout the world. That is why the introduction and success of the Euro was controversial and scrutinized.

This is the backdrop that Chris Donaldson is trying to navigate, where the White House demanded him to stop criminal use of cryptocurrency but apart from eliminating cryptocurrency altogether, he could not do what they asked. There will always be criminals and if it wasn't cryptocurrency there would be something else or revert to heavier reliance on weapons or drugs as currency to finance their crime or the

U.S. dollar itself. The U.S. dollar is a favorite among criminals. He could not stop all criminals and yes cryptocurrency may make the transfer of money procured by illegal means, but cryptocurrency did have legitimate purposes. Technology, innovation, and development cannot be contained for the good guys. Although Chris wished it could.

The last SEC Chairman, Chris' boss, did not get the results the White House wanted, and that is why he was let go. Well officially he resigned. So now, Chris is acting SEC Chairman and he is inheriting the Locke Market investigation case.

The Locke Market is designed to enable users to engage in transactions and communications anonymously. All Locke Market users are required to transact in cryptocurrencies, no official government backed currencies. Locke hosts more than one million users and 5,000 vendors.

A recent whistle-blower revelation to the media on the FBI's use of a new tool, the network investigative technique (NIT) in the Locke Market investigation got immense backlash. A NIT required the stamp of approval from a judge, which allowed the FBI to essentially hack all computers that access a particular website. There was immense public backlash, especially because many felt a judge approval is just a formality and NIT applications for a warrant are guaranteed to receive judge approval.

The way a NIT works is a virus is sent to a computer that has been assigned a unique identifier for accessing the target website. Upon activation of the virus, which can be sent in various forms, the virus automatically searches the computer to collect the computer's IP address and identifying information. This information is then seized by the virus and sent back to the government. NITs are generally deployed after the government has already secured control over the website or the host server of the website.

There are complaints that the Fourth Amendment warrant requirement did not allow this type of broad dragnet search and seizure of any and everyone's computers across the country. But the Bureau had snuck this change into the warrant procedures nearly two years ago in an amendment to the federal rules of criminal procedure forty-one. And like in Washington D.C. true fashion, civil rights activists complained and there were a couple of social media petitions. But after that frenzy died with a new issue in the media, Congress no longer cared about the civil rights implications, and the public was never the wiser. Criminal defense attorney's continued to challenge in cases and some judges cautioned the FBI, nevertheless, the FBI kept trudging along applying for warrants to the NIT, until the leak.

The Locke Market is used to communicate freely, anonymously, and securely by activists, community organizers and journalists around the world. To share and transfer journalist documentation, reports on human rights abuses, information from interviews and pictures inside war torn and/or oppressive regime countries and sending money to support humanitarian aid groups and journalists, activists and lawyers' efforts on the ground in these countries. And the NIT violated these individuals and entities reasonable expectation of privacy. These individuals and groups by their very actions of operating on Locke meant they had taken deliberate steps to remain anonymous and private. But now the government had intruded on their privacy without probable cause because there was no individualized proof that they had engaged in a criminal act.

The FBI's NIT also threatened the security and safety of these individuals and groups, whose identity was only protected by their anonymity. And as the leaked show, the risk of their information, existence and identity becoming known to bad actors that opposed their actions is real. Locke was being used to share information by and on lawyers who were being targeted and arrested in China, activists killed in Syria, and journalists imprisoned in Myanmar. The public was outraged when the warrant documents authorizing the NIT were revealed.

Nearly eighty-six percent of the Locke Market users are using the platform for legitimate purposes. But Locke also enabled the other fourteen percent of users to buy and sell illegal goods and services, including controlled substances, stolen and fraudulent identification documents and devices, counterfeit goods, money laundering, malware and other computer hacking tools, firearms, and toxic chemicals. Locke derived hundreds of millions of dollars from these illegal transactions. Locke also takes a percentage of the purchase price as a commission, between two percent and six percent, on the illegal transactions conducted through its website. The operators and employees of the site controlled and profited from those commissions, which were worth at least tens of millions of dollars. So far, their investigation had focused on finding the website owner to get the crypto to no avail.

The Locke Market only exists on the dark web, meaning it is accessible only through The Onion Router (Tor) network, which makes the Internet Protocol (IP) addresses of its underlying servers anonymous. Tor is a free internet browser that allows users to use the internet anonymously. Tor is used just like any other internet browsing platform except Tor is a global decentralized system. Tor was originally designed, implemented, and deployed as a product of the U.S. Naval Research Laboratory for the primary purpose of protecting government communications. The Tor software protects users' privacy online by bouncing their communications around a distributed network of relay computers run by volunteers all around the world, thereby masking the user's actual IP address which could otherwise be used to identify a user. It's a network of computers across the internet that function as multilayer conduits, known as nodes, for your internet use as the sender and the end receiver. The computers in the network of relay computers know the time and date it receives communication but with end to end encryption on each layer, the computer nodes do not know the content of your internet traffic nor who is the original sender or ultimate receiver. Encryption is deployed throughout the Tor network from the entry guard nodes through the relay. It does not know where the communication is going or the true IP address of the user. The nodes are randomly selected from all over the world and make it seem as if you are on a website in Portugal, when you are really in California because your internet traffic is routed through their computer. Essentially it is protecting your Internet address, your location, and identity. This aids in the anonymity of the network. It prevents someone attempting to monitor an Internet connection from learning what sites a user visits, prevents the true physical locations of the website's administrators, moderators, and users, and it lets the user access sites which could otherwise be blocked. Thus, Chris knows it will be difficult to trace the cryptocurrency to the actual bad actors when deploying the NIT. Even with the government's control of the website server and hacking of website user computers, this did not tell us where the money had gone. Whether it had been stored in a crypto-bank or cashed in through a crypto-exchange. Locke requires its users, both vendors and buyers, to execute transactions through digital currency addresses hosted and ultimately controlled by the site, not the user. These digital currency addresses are outside of the Locke platform, and have barriers in place to deny access to even vendors.

Cryptocurrency was not created with the intent to facilitate crime, but it was being used for crime, because nobody thought it could be regulated. And Locke users once identified faced drug and money laundering charges. The FBI had already been operating the Locke investigation for nearly two years when Chris became acting SEC Chairman.

The person behind the criminal network exploiting and hacking the Locke Market, he is hard at work or maybe she is hard at work. Women are just as capable with the education qualifications, intelligence, and skill set to excel and innovate in the tech financial industry. Women are cyber security experts, coders, computer programmers, cryptologists, hackers, and the list goes on. The bias toward women and people of color in the financial and technology industries crept in often, even here at the SEC. The bias is reflected in the tech financial industry, mostly composed of white men. Asian and South Asian men had a significant presence, but women and people of color are seemingly cut out. But that didn't matter anyway. As the FBI explained it to Chris, they are dealing with a highly organized individual or groups of individuals that had coordinated an online criminal trafficking operation. That is all the information given, even after a slew of questions.

The FBI made clear that this is their investigation, they were in charge, and they were not sharing, so much for the 9/11 commission recommendations. To be fair this was more than just a white-collar crime and the SEC is not a national security agency. But the impact of cryptocurrency in the marketplace and thus the stability of the U.S. economy is a domestic security concern. Chris should not have expected anything more from them. They only formalized this joint operation to use the SEC. They needed the SEC's expertise in cryptocurrency to understand how cryptocurrency was potentially working on the Locke Market. To stop the Locke Market and other websites that would pop up to fulfill the supply and demand, when the Locke Market was shutdown.

The FBI's handling of the case was anticipated. The heat on the FBI was amplified due to recent reports that Locke Market is a major source of drugs, particularly opioids. The opioid addiction has created widespread panic by the rich and powerful. That is why we were here. Bitcoin was being used in the sale and transaction of opioids to middle- and upper-class America through the Locke Market. The FBI got the NIT and acted.

Uniformed FBI agents decked out in bulletproof vests and swat gear raided the home of Locke Market website username Bl@cqKn!ght95. A woman in the home is arrested and brought in for questioning. In the grey stone interrogation room, she sits with her hands handcuffed at a steel desk.

"I do not know who is using my IP address. But I am telling you that I am not involved in any drugs." Lar states.

"Why are you using the website then? Can you explain that?" The FBI interrogator asks.

"I use it to pay my computer programmers overseas. Women who are not allowed to have bank accounts. I am using the platform to mask these payments for their work to protect them." Lars answers.

"We have seized your computers, electronic devices, hard drives, and you want to know what I think they are going to tell us? That you are directly involved, your fingerprints on everything and we will find the opioids and the drug money." The FBI interrogator states.

Lars just looks at him and states, "I am exercising my right to remain silent."

The FBI interrogator laughs, "Okay if that is the way you want to play it then fine!" He slams his fist on the steel table. "Grand jury indictments are forthcoming, followed by prosecutions. Information obtained from Bl@cqKn!ght95's hard drive, your hard drive."

"Like I said…"

The FBI interrogator interrupts Lars, "I am done listening, if you are not going to tell me the truth. The hard drive that was seized during the raid, points to the involvement of persons in South Africa. Who do you know in South Africa? Is that where the drugs are coming from?! Or is that where the money is hidden?!"

"I am trying to tell you. But you don't want to listen. You are not hearing me. You have already decided the narrative and determined to see I fit the narrative no matter what. This is not an investigation! You are trying to get me to admit to something that I have not done, and I will not!" Lars responds.

"I am supposed to take your word over the resources and intelligence of the FBI?" He asks Lars.

"Look. I am just trying to get women who are oppressed an opportunity to make a better life for themselves through economic freedom. That's it. Nothing more, nothing less. The Locke Market provides a secure network to do that." Lars replies.

"Why do this is you are not involved in illegal activity. And if you are not involved, then give us the women's names?" He asks Lars.

"I don't think you understand, that these women lives are at risk if their husbands find out they are working and hiding money from them. They do not have the freedom we have. I cannot give you their names. You cannot guarantee their security." Lars replies.

"You expect me to believe that you are out here just using a website known to be involved in illegal activity to pay your employees with Bitcoin? Cryptocurrency that is untraceable?" He asks Lars.

"Bitcoin doesn't change the amount of criminality. Guess what 20 years ago, we had transactions that were not tracked. It's called cash. The aspect that the government should be able to track transactions and they can't with crypto currency is bullshit. Criminals use banks. How do you think anti-money laundering works?" Lars replies.

"Okay, clearly we are done here." The FBI interrogator states and leaves the room.

The FBI contacts the South African national law enforcement authorities. The FBI needs to engage in a coordinated effort to question individuals linked to IP addresses in South Africa back to New York to face interrogation and potentially prosecution. The other option is depending upon the willingness of the South African authorities, the South African authorities can open their own investigation into the individuals and share any information found with the FBI. The individuals could then face prosecution on separate charges in South Africa too. The fate of Lars and the women she swore to protect weighed in the balance.

CHAPTER 9

A PIECE OF THE PIE

———

This is the call Joe was waiting on. The call from the Department of Justice Assistant telling him that the judge ordered Eclipse to give the IRS their records on about 15,000 customers who bought, sold, sent, or received at least $20,000 value of cryptocurrency in 2013, 2014, and 2015.

"This is great to hear." Joe said. "Will this be shared outside the agency?" Joe asks.

The Assistant U.S. Attorney responds to Joe, "Everything will go through the proper channels. If a crime or violation of law is found, we will be sure to inform the proper authorities and share any information at that time."

"I understand. Do please reach out to me for anything." Joe replies.

"It's good to hear that. I was actually calling as a professional courtesy, as we are going to need your office cooperation." The Assistant U.S. Attorney replied.

"What do you mean?" Joe asked.

"Well let's begin with just the basic information. We are going to need any case files you may have on Eclipse or investigation related to Eclipse." the Assistant U.S. Attorney states.

Joe chuckles. "Why not just make a formal agency request? We have those procedures laid out in the interagency memos of understanding for things like this for a reason. And you strike as a straight shooter. So why the secretive actions, what are you or the agency trying to hide?" Joe asks.

"Not hiding anything. Just sometimes have to color outside the lines for the greater good. Look at this time there is a lot of red tape over here, won't be able to get permission from my superiors to even send the request. It's different if your agency says no and rejects it. But it's my people over here saying no. What I'm on to is big, I think it's connected and someone, with some connections and power, doesn't want me to connect the dots. That's why they are blocking my formal request from even being considered." the Assistant U.S. Attorney states.

"Look I get it. But what you are asking for. That is not possible. If you are looking for something specific, I can check for you. If I find something, then maybe I can get approval to share that specific information, maybe." Joe responds.

"Then its best we meet in person to discuss in more detail. I'm calling from a secure line, but you never know. Call probably being monitored." The Assistant U.S. Attorney responds.

"Okay. See you then." Joe hangs up the phone and goes back to work.

He looks up the court order in the Eclipse case online. The court order was based on discrepancies between Eclipse users and U.S. citizens reporting Bitcoin gains to the IRS. Eclipse and their customers engaged in mass tax evasion to the tune of about $4 million. Eclipse is a massive cryptocurrency trading exchange platform that allows investors to convert their virtual currency holdings back into U.S. dollars. Bitcoin is the primary cryptocurrency used on the platform, and hence the reason why Eclipse is under the IRS microscope. Eclipse is not just operational in the United States, but around the world. Which means this case and legal fight is going to be subject to scrutiny by foreign governments and businesses. The world is watching how the United States handles Eclipse.

The IRS rules seem simple, if you make a profit, pay for services or goods, or sell property it's taxable income that must be reported to the IRS. Whether virtual currency or fiat currency, currency is currency and just like the U.S. dollar is subject to U.S. income tax laws, which makes profits from investments in virtual currency, assets, networks, or economies taxable income too. For example, if you purchased

Bitcoin for five dollars per GoinCold and now Bitcoin is valued at one-hundred dollars per Bitcoin and you sell or exchange that Bitcoin for U.S. dollar, the ninety-five-dollar difference that you earned is subject to tax. Every single transaction, even profit on one Bitcoin is taxable income.

However, most people do not know the regular tax requirements as to fiat currency and now the IRS is expecting people to know how the tax code applies to virtual currencies. There is no separate cryptocurrency reporting IRS form and the IRS did not do a good job on informing the public. So how could Mike, Sam, and the public know what to do, and understand the technical filing rules of how cryptocurrency gains should be characterized and counted? A different percentage is taxed depending on if the cryptocurrency was held for a short term or long-term period. If short term, the crypto is taxed as "ordinary income" as part of your standard income tax bracket. But if long term, the crypto is taxed at zero, fifteen, or twenty percent depending on your income.

The court order in the IRS case against Eclipse makes it seem that tax evasion is so rampant now because of cryptocurrency. But the truth is that tax evasion has occurred since the beginning of Uncle Sam's, the IRS creation. There are plenty of people that don't report their complete income, failed to pay taxes, or failed to file taxes at all before cryptocurrency. Even now, most of these same tax evaders likely don't own cryptocurrency now. They own regular securities and stock. But the IRS placed tax evaders in one of three categories. First: the unskilled, undocumented, or returning citizens (persons formerly incarcerated) that only could earn a living getting paid for temporary, usually physically intensive labor, the money under the table type of jobs. The CFTC was not really worried about those that fell into this group. The second category is made up of individuals whose income is illegally obtained and tied to a crime. There is no paper trail, no pay stubs, and no bank accounts. The second category is a priority for criminal enforcement agencies and the IRS with law enforcement interests taking priority over the IRS interests. The third category is the white-collar criminal, dressed in fancy suits, behind glass marble desks, in offices with Ivy League degrees hanging on the wall. They have hundreds of thousands in the bank, likely millions hidden somewhere overseas in Panama or London. They have the top accountants, the best lawyers backed by massive firms with impeccable reach and influence. Yes, this is the priority, the SEC and CFTC'S priority, Joe's priority. This third group spoke the compliance and good business owner lingo, a career criminal that could operate in plain sight, the wealthy businessman.

"Hey Joe, someone from the Department of Justice is at the front." A colleague said to him.

"Who?" Joe asks.

The colleague responds, "Didn't say. It's a woman though."

Joe makes his way to the front of the office. He sees a woman in a suit. Government issued name tag on her suit jacket. He walks back to his boss's office. Joe knocks on the door, "Sir, can I bother you for a second of your time?" The CFTC chairman waves him in.

"I got a call from the Department of Justice earlier today, an Assistant U.S. Attorney. She talked briefly to me about the Eclipse matter. You know the recent court order demanding Eclipse hand over user information to the IRS." Joe is standing near the door, only maybe a foot in the office.

The CFTC Chairman interrupts him. Not looking up, he speaks "Yea. I heard about it. So?", signing his name on documents that he hands to his assistant.

Joe resumes speaking, "Well she said she wanted information related to any investigation we may have on Eclipse. I am not working on anything related to Eclipse. I didn't say we had anything to her, but I was wondering if you or maybe someone else did?"

"You would be informed if there was something that you should know. You try to find out as much as you can about what the Department of Justice and IRS know. Don't tell her anything, you hear me?" the CFTC Chairman states.

"I understand. I just think it would be helpful if we all were on the same page if we were looking into Eclipse too." Joe responds.

The CFTC Chairman responds, "Not your concern."

Joe takes the CFTC Chairman statement as his que to stop talking and leave. He leaves and heads back to the front of the office. On his walk there, Joe thought maybe the Assistant U.S. Attorney was right about people higher up in the agency not wanting anyone asking about Eclipse. The CFTC Chairman had swiftly shutdown his questioning about it. Or it could be that any investigation was classified as highly confidential and the details were supposed to be kept between a few key people to protect the investigation and prevent leaks. The less people privy to certain information the better may be their higher ups thinking.

Joe approaches her, "You're looking for me?"

She responds, "Maybe. Joe Meija."

"That is me." Joe responds.

"I'm the Assistant U.S. Attorney you spoke with on the phone earlier today." She responds.

Joe replies. "Yes. I'm sorry I kept you waiting. I was in the middle of working on something due when you came. I didn't expect you so soon. I didn't know you meant today when you said we should speak in person."

The Assistant U.S. Attorney shifts her brief case from one hand to the other. "I'd like to get it handled right away if possible." She states.

"Okay." Joe responds.

"Is there some place we can speak privately?" The Assistant U.S. Attorney asks Joe.

"Let's see what I can find. Rooms get booked up quickly around here. I'm sure you know. Space is precious over at Department of Justice too I can imagine." Joe states.

"Yes, a commodity." the Assistant U.S. Attorney smirks.

"Good one." Joe pulls aside an associate to ask about a room. He turns back to the Assistant U.S. Attorney, "this way please." Joe heads down a hallway. The Assistant U.S. Attorney follows him. They make a right, down the stairs, across the room. They enter the third room on the left. Joe holds the door open for the Assistant U.S. Attorney, "Here we are." Joe tells her.

"I wanted to talk to you in person about Eclipse. So that you can understand how sensitive this matter is." says the Assistant U.S. Attorney.

"I appreciate that and the sensitivity of the matter." Joe responds.

The Assistant U.S. Attorney continues speaking, "Now, we have been monitoring the virtual currency brokerage firm, Eclipse, for some time. They were reporting just enough income to not raise alarms, engaged in transactions just under the $10,000 radar. No alarms, but there were flags and we were watching ever more closely when news reports that one of the biggest cryptocurrency exchanges is valued at over 200 billion and made their customers over fifty billion this past year. But not one reported in last year's tax returns filed with the IRS of earnings tied to this million-dollar company. This is when we started digging."

"The company executives could be lying to the public." Joe states.

"Or their wealthy customers, cryptocurrency traders, were lying to the IRS." The Assistant U.S. Attorney states.

She opens her brief case and takes a file out. She opens the
file and begins to show the file documents to Joe, spreading
them out on the table.

Joe is quickly glancing over the documents. There is a
list compiled together from an excel sheet. He notices that
any transaction that is $2,000 or more is highlighted in yel-
low. "This is all about fraud?" Joe asks, putting pages behind
the other as he finishes reviewing them.

"It is a crime. And it is my job to prosecute crime."
She states.

"That's not it. There is something more the Department
of Justice is after. Is there another case this is tied to? Or are
you targeting someone on this list specifically?" Joe asks.

The Assistant U.S. Attorney responds, "There is no ulterior motive. Cryptocurrency is a big deal and we got to get
ahead of this thing. It can be exploited by nefarious actors,
and no one wants that."

"You are going to prosecute someone for earning $2,000
in crypto?" Joe asks.

"How about we change to why I came to speak with you,
a specific request. The Department of Justice wants to see if
you may be able to provide information on BC Trusts. The
company came up a few times in our inquiries." the Assistant
U.S. Attorney states.

"Fraud is happening everywhere. Most of these users
you know are going to be low to middle class. You're not
going to get those with significant Bitcoin that really can

influence the market with a sale, transfer, or purpose. If you want those who essentially control the market because significant market share of the Bitcoin's out there, this is not the way." Joe states.

She responds. "Either way, they are committing fraud and the administration is determined to hold them all accountable."

"The administration, oh this is about sending a message?" asks Joe.

"Joe, criminals are using these virtual platforms. Terrorists, there is a real danger." She states looking him in his eyes.

"These people in your IRS documents are not terrorists. And you know that." Joe states.

"No, I don't. And neither do you. So, what shall you have me do?" She smirks at him.

"What is your lawyer's favorite term, selective prosecution," Joe states.

"Look, I wish we could remove all bad actors and those that seek to manipulate the crypto-market, so that people who rely on crypto-market can do so knowing that it's fair. There are a lot of scammers, but even good people must follow the rules. And when they don't follow the rules, they become bad actors." She responds.

"You can't even say that with a straight face." Joe states.

"We have to strictly enforce the law or people will continue to evade the law, and I will be right back here prosecuting more and more people for tax evasion." She responds.

"You actually believe that?" Joe replies.

"The law says I must prosecute. Not me. I don't like this anymore than you. I'm just a tiny nail in the machine." She states.

"Oh, so you're not responsible right. This is not everything you dreamed of when you were in law school. I'm sorry to hear that. But this is your job. You can do it well or you can do it right. Just exercise discretion. The real criminals, the terrorists will always find a way to get around. Those are the people we are actually after don't get in the way of that, while the people that actually face prosecution are not criminals." Joe gets up. "And as for your request, I think not. It doesn't seem that the CFTC has any information on that." Joe leaves the room.

Walking across the room, thoughts run through Joe's mind. He doesn't know if he should have said any of that or talked to the Assistant U.S. Attorney in that way. "What is she going to do?" He thought. "I made a mistake maybe I should go back and explain." Joe stops walking and looks back.

The white-collar criminals outmaneuver the IRS. They always have and always will. Developing elaborate schemes to avoid paying taxes and avoid reporting income. Using the complex tax system rules and foreign privacy and bank laws to hide their wealth they would report some of their income, but not all. And when you are working with billions of dollars, even a meager five percent of income unreported over a period of time, can add up to millions. The IRS can't stop them. They would continue to evade reporting and paying taxes. Meanwhile the Department of Justice goes after the couple who profited a few thousand with the power of the state, not the monopoly that has evaded paying millions in taxes every year for over a decade. For what, he thought.

The IRS is not naive. They know all about the various tax system schemes and tax liability exceptions that allow tax evasion to perpetuate, because it is technically not illegal. And this is set up by design not to be illegal, to benefit the white-collar criminal because the white-collar criminal's money and power made it so. The Department of Justice just got lucky with this Eclipse court order and wants to turn up the pressure. The Department of Justice is pushing news articles, press conferences, interviews, all the works that government resources can bear on Eclipse. This type of pressure is a tool to force others to talk to them and make deals to obtain information on others in exchange for lesser penalties. While the Department of Justice hands may be tied and focused on getting as many prosecutions and settlements as possible, just to save face, the CFTC hands were not.

* * *

They all had been waiting on a decision from the SEC. They thought any day now, as the SEC had set the deadline for this month. But that did not happen. Brad receives word from the Gallagher Firm that the SEC is delaying their decision on Eclipse. The SEC sets a new deadline to allow the commission more time to review Eclipse in consideration of new proposed rules.

Eclipse is not the only crypto company the SEC is watching. Since the SEC's announcement on its inquiry into Eclipse, the SEC has opened numerous inquiries and investigations into other crypto companies. They have made settlements on all of them. All except Eclipse. It was clear that the SEC had no intention of taking them to court. Well really the Department of Justice, because the Department of Justice, not the SEC would file the lawsuit. The SEC just investigates. The SEC uses tools of manipulation and intimidation to try and get Eclipse to the negotiation table. SEC's intent was to make Eclipse and those associated with Eclipse scared, but all that the SEC showed was that the Department of Justice was scared to prosecute this case. That is why the IRS subpoena for records came. If the IRS can show that crypto holders did not report income when they should have, that's an easier case to prosecute then allegedly securities fraud, assuming they are able to prove to a court that the crypto asset in question is a security.

"What are they going to find when they get those records from Eclipse? Are they are asking for BC Trusts records too as their associate? Executive officers at Eclipse called us. Are we liable?" Sean asks Brad.

Moto talks over Brad. "Well we don't have to hand over the records. I know Gallagher Firm advises we give it to the government. But we can push this issue and spin the narrative about government intrusion with the media. That will show our clients that we are serious about them protecting their data and personal information. That we really care about our customers and value their privacy."

"I mean we challenged the government's request, there is nowhere else to go from here. It's in our best interests to comply." Brad states.

"I do not want to hear that. We are going to fight it. Let's put those high-priced attorney's to good use. We cannot cave in now, and go to our customers, investors, and board, and say oh we tried, and we failed. No! We will appeal the court order and take this case to the court of public opinion. This is about our right to privacy not about curtailing innovation and intrusion on people's livelihood and access to opportunity." Moto responds.

"Moto that is easy for you to say. But I got a letter from the IRS. They are coming after me for a few thousand. It's not even about the money. This is going to impact future tax filings and other financial related transactions. When I'm trying to get a credit card, buy a house or car, future tax filings. I'm going to be under a microscope, scrutinized for the rest of my life." Sam states.

"They already got Sam. The IRS knows that Sam is a partner at BC Trusts, and we have a significant holding in Eclipse. They're not stupid. If we don't cooperate, we are setting ourselves up for more scrutiny. Our office and homes can be raided. Our families and friends interrogated. Our financial assets frozen and our reputation individually and BC Trusts ruined by the press surrounding this. I don't see a way out of this. We have to comply." Sean states.

"I'm actually surprised at you Sean. The person who was adamant that we not even acknowledge anything or do anything with the Mt. X scandal because we are not responsible for the actions of others," states Moto.

"This is different. This is the federal government taking action against us." Sean states.

"No, it's the same here. We have no control over whether people pay their taxes or not and cannot be blamed for that. We did not tell people to violate the law or not report their sales or transactions as income. I mean what are we really supposed to do? Our customers trust, and thus anonymity is the heart of our business. What are we going to do now? What does this do to our business if the court is ordering us to breach the confidentiality and trust of our customers?" Moto asks.

"We may want to think about taking BC Trusts overseas, perhaps Singapore, Malta, England, or Africa. The laws are much friendlier toward ICOs and tokens." said Brad.

Moto replies, "No. They are not going to bully us out of our own country. And they cannot create rules as they go and then say you should have followed them. We did nothing illegal. It's not right."

"I don't think this IRS rule on cryptocurrency reporting is actually new. Most people may not know about it or understand it. Or thought we as third parties would have to report. But it doesn't matter because ignorance of the law is not a defense. It doesn't make the rules not apply. They still apply to us." Brad states.

Sean responds, "The priority is maximizing our opportunities overseas in this industry and limiting our exposure to U.S. regulation, but still maintaining compliance with U.S. law where necessary. I know you want to see what we built to succeed."

"No, I built this! And I am not going to roll over. This all started with blockchain and my work. And all you did is lie, cheat, and steal. Because that is the only way you do things just to be on top. You did this!" Moto states.

"What are you talking about?!" Sean stammers.

"All you care about is money and success. You turned this into a business. That is all you have always cared about. That is why we are here, just selfish!" Moto states.

"This is a business, I told you that before. I didn't ask you to join BC Trusts and if you don't want to be a part of it, which is clear because you run at the first sign of trouble like at the Gallagher firm. You know me. I have never hid being good in business and striving for success. There is no point in having a business if it's not a successful one. It's not a bad thing. I don't know or understand where all this is coming from?!" Sean states.

"It's your ambition, it ruins everything. I know you took my blockchain paper and posted it on the internet. It was you who shared my work without my permission, chasing success. I know and I did not forget." Moto walks toward Sean.

"Bitcoin was not supposed to be all this crap. Trusts, exchanges, stock. This is for the rich." Moto throws his hands up in the air. "And that is why we are here. Because we have lost our way and strayed from our purpose that is for the people cut out of access to wealth not the rich. You can see that right Sam?" Moto looks at Sam.

Moto turns his attention back to Sean. "And you want to feel important, you need it to survive. For you this is all about revenge, showing corporate America up, your old bosses and friends who dumped you and fired you when you were no longer one of them. I don't trust you. If you are going down, you are going down by yourself and you have no one else to blame but yourself." Moto stares at Sean.

"It's actually a little sad. I feel sorry for you. Maybe you can have some dignity and not take Sam and Brad down with you!" Moto states.

Moto gets up to walk out.

"Where are you going?" Sam asks.

"I don't need to be here. Clearly you guys, the board, have made your decision on this. I don't need to be here. I don't agree and it may be time for me and Sam to dissolve this partnership. Boards are supposed to advise, and partners are supposed to decide. But that is not what is happening here Sam. And that is why I gave you those conditions from the beginning, Sam. Because this is not just a business for me, so I want out, out of BC Trusts, out of it all. It's time for me to go off the grid. Start something on my own." Moto replies and slams the door.

Brad, Sam, and Sean look at each other in disbelief.

All cryptocurrency holders are on notice, that for all intents and purposes the IRS classifies cryptocurrency as property, and the sale of such property for a profit is taxable. If you fail to abide by the IRS rules, and fail to report these profits as income the IRS will come after you for every Bitcoin.

The IRS knows the future will have government backed currency co-existing and competing alongside Bitcoin, virtual currency with distributed ledgers, powered by math, electricity, and the people. Yes, Uncle Sam knows this, and he wants his cut.

PART III

"*I hope this technology will prove useful, particularly in helping people who are unbanked or underserved by the traditional financial system...*"

—U.S. SENATOR SHERROD BROWN

CHAPTER 10

DARK NET CORRUPT

___

The intercom sounds, and the soft MLK cheerful voice of the stewardess is a welcomed interruption.

"Welcome to South Africa. On behalf of the airlines, pilot, and crew, we thank you for flying with us. We know that you could have flown with any airline, so we truly appreciate you choosing to fly with us today. We are at gate eleven and for those who have checked baggage you can pick up your baggage at carousel two. For those who had their luggage checked at the gate, your luggage will be right outside to the left when you depart the plane. Be mindful when removing your baggage from the overhead bin as some of the items could have shifted during flight." The stewardess said.

Chris's security detail sitting in the window seat lifts the window shade and the sun's brightness fully wakes

Chris from his insomnia. The sun is permeating through the window.

The plane trip is not too bad in business class. The original flight was delayed, so he had to book the next flight out of Malta to South Africa in economy class. No one recognized Chris, the SEC Chairman, on the flight. Everyone was either heading to or coming from a vacation. That was their focus and he did not mind.

Ding.

The pilot turns off the seat belt safety alert and you hear seat belts un-click. Chaos ensues. Everyone is up, holding onto their personal belongings and maybe passing one to two seats in front of them, before the inevitable airplane departure waiting. Fifteen minutes later, people are still waiting. A few are tapping their fingers; Chris sees many people take a deep breath followed by releases where you see their chest go up and down. A few women in heels shift their weight from one foot to the other.

Despite this, the woman sitting in the passenger seat next him looking at him impatiently, Chris remains seated. What should he do? Try to stand and bend his body over the seat in front of him to avoid hitting his head on the overhead compartment and get a crank in his neck? For what, they clearly were not going anywhere. He just smiled and took his phone out of his pocket to check his calls and text messages.

The heat hits him as he walks down the steps from the plane to the tarmac, hits him like he's walking into a sauna and its 108 degrees. That dry heat but he can feel the beauty of the country already. He sees trees and hears the beating of drums. As he exits the airport, he's swarmed with taxi drivers trying to convince him to get in their car. They are asking him where he's going and telling him they will give him a good deal.

His assistant Mitch was prepared to deal with the hagglers, but Mitch is not here with him. Mitch warned Chris that the hagglers would spot him by his American clothing, mannerisms, and accent. And even beyond that, Mitch said they would know based on the flight arrival information that was posted at the airport terminals the incoming flights from the United States and corresponding with his exit from the arrival terminal. Mitch may have thought otherwise and told Chris how to avoid the hagglers. To Chris, he appreciated the business skills at work. This was an example of pulling resources to gather information to understand the customers' needs, wants, and expectations.

This is great, Chris thought. Not too many places left in the world where you can still haggle. The people are full of life, energy, and hustle. Is this what attracted so many to Bitcoin Investments or better known as Nguzo Saba in South Africa. The hustle and energy of Nguzo Saba sure enough had a vision. Straight robbery, the people had to know it was a risk. But did they? The culture is to hustle to make it in South Africa where every day involves risk taking. Did they really understand the risk if this is how life is?

Like clockwork, Chris' security detail hands him his Android phone and tells him, "It's your assistant, Mitch."

He could barely say hello before Mitch launched into full de-brief mode. "You have your itinerary for today and tomorrow, correct? If you do not, I have emailed you a copy. I will also be in touch with you and your security 24/7, updating the security about fifteen minutes before your next appointment or meeting on the schedule. There is not much on the schedule tonight, just the keynote speech at the conference. You should be in route to the convention center now Chairman. Are you in route?"

"Yes, I am getting in the car now." Chris answers Mitch.

"Good. Remember what I said about hagglers. And after the keynote speech, there will be a private dinner for you to attend with financial tech industry stakeholders. South African and other foreign government officials may be in attendance. I will arrive in South Africa tomorrow at 7:00 a.m. and will meet you at your 8:00 morning briefing. Again Chairman, I apologize for not being there now with you today. Family dynamics are complicated, but they need me right now." Mitch states.

"Don't worry about it Mitch. I will see you tomorrow, and do not forget to bring the hard copies of the Locke Market report findings." Chris states.

"Of course, Chairman." Mitch responds

Call ends.

Chris, as the SEC Chairmen, is in South Africa to try to use the Bitcoin Investments scandal as an opportunity to build on diplomatic relations in technology development. He is here to educate the country on how all their citizens got ripped off, the government officials that fell asleep at the wheel, and the companies, the ones that survived, that were barely hanging on to air. The attendees are investors, regulators, and finance professionals. This would make up the financial technology conference audience that he would give his keynote speech to. He planned to lecture, somewhat nicely scold, but mostly inspire conference attendees about how the U.S. position on utility tokens and mediums of exchange, and regulation of digital securities, cryptocurrencies, initial coin offerings, and coin exchange platforms.

Dozens of companies, who invested Nguzo Saba and employed hundreds, would be at the conference. These companies that now built their own token-based platforms are trying to regain the trust of their customers and their presence at the conference is a step toward this goal. The work of regaining their customer's trust is difficult for some companies to understand. This was South Africa, everyone knew that everything had a price, to keep the water and electricity on you grease the pockets of the official that bills your usage. In order to get the building permit for the new school and community center, palms must be greased, and so on. If you do not, you and your family go without the basic necessities like water, electricity, and the habitable living conditions that water and electricity provide like heat, preserving and cooking food, and your children will go without education, access, and opportunity.

Yes, Chris planned to shed light on how corruption is a disease and had seeped into the crypto investment Ponzi scheme Nguzo Saba. Corruption is the root of the problem it was not the technology itself. Blockchain technology could assist South African businesses and the country in economic development, especially in industries lacking institutional investment. Digital assets and cryptocurrency also had a place. Corruption infested the country, the very soil and air the South African people stood on and breathed decades before. If every basic transaction on a daily basis essentially involved a bribe, stolen funds, or misuse of funds, then why would Nguzo Saba be any different?

As Chris walks into the hotel conference room, he is immediately greeted by the cool air conditioner. He hears the sounds of shoes and heels on the marble hotel floor. A few of the conference volunteers at the registration desk rush over to him and his security detail holds them off. Chris is escorted to a private room to discuss the speaker details with the conference organizers. After going over the details, they quickly rush him to the main ballroom where the keynote is scheduled, along with lunch. The clink of wine glasses gets everyone's attention.

"Please give a warm welcome to the SEC Chairman, Chris Donaldson."

Applause.

He is so preoccupied going over his notes that he misses the master of ceremonies announce his name as Keynote Speaker. The conference organizers nudge him between claps and smile to get Chris's attention. They point to the stage and whisper, "They called your name." Chris gets up and walks up the steps to the stage podium.

"Thank you for welcoming me. More than ever, we live in an interconnected and co-dependent world. Innovation and technology have allowed us to exceed our biggest dreams and ideas we never thought possible. From the internet to FaceTime, GPS to solar cars, we have used technology to propel our societies forward. Allowing us to touch people all around the world quickly and efficiently, and make a better life, a greater future for generations to come. This has not been more profound than in the financial marketplace. South Africa is more than just an emerging market, but a regional leader in fintech."

Chris pauses for applause before continuing to speak.

"A leader in fintech holds great power to transform the way the industry thinks, but most importantly the future policies that will manage this great power. Technology and innovation should be encouraged. We do not have to look any further for this inspiration, than BitTransparency. BitTransparency is a company operating in Ghana that has utilized the blockchain technology to expedite the processing of humanitarian aid and tracking how that aid is dispersed and used, down to the details of the supplies and laborers needed. In one project, the building of a well. BitTransparency provided a direct line of the humanitarian aid to directly buy the bricks that were used to build the well. This demonstrates that innovation and security are not mutually exclusive. With great power there is great responsibility. And that great responsibility weighs on the shoulders of governments and government officials. And we have to be sharp, because there are those in the darknet that want to exploit technology for their own mischievous gain and to commit crimes, to bestow fear and sow mistrust in the economy, government, and society. That is why the United States top priority in the digital asset cryptocurrency market is to rid the marketplace of fraud and manipulation to protect investors. Why you ask? Because the traditional notion of an investor is no longer a bank, billion dollar company, or state institution, it is your grandmother who worked all her life raising her grandchildren by working as a maid, your daughter who is dreaming of going to college, and your son whom is trying to get his small business off the ground. They look at cryptocurrency and see the opportunity for their future as endless, the opportunity for their children, the opportunity to reinvigorate the middle class, and help millions out of poverty. The same access and opportunity that enabled the barriers to investment, development, and matriculation of wealth to be broken down through cryptocurrency and blockchain, now threaten those very same traditionally disadvantaged populations that see cryptocurrency as digital gold. If we sit idly by, they will take the hard-earned money of the working poor, the grandmother's retirement savings, the student's school payments, the mortgage and rent payments, literally everything, without a second thought."

Chris pauses. He sees attendees nodding their head in agreement.

"We have to protect the grandmother, the student. We must put in mechanisms that ensure oversight, accountability, and transparency. If a company is offering a digital security, they must be subject to mandatory registration, regulation, and public disclosure on risks, assets, corporate structure. A digital security can be found where there is: 1) an investment or a request for money, capital, and/or assets to help build or create a tangible digital product like an application, and in exchange receive interest; 2) perhaps a token that can be cashed in for fiat currency, or used to receive a good or service, or where expectation that the investor will be able to benefit somehow from the application, whether monetarily or through use and/or access to the platform. The importance of this work is ever more present right here in South Africa, where not too long ago the Nguzo Saba coin was exposed as a Ponzi scheme. A company operating in the shadows but publicly available for investment at the same time, using the decentralization built into blockchain technology and using the anonymity built into cryptocurrency transactions, to steal money from our grandmother, our children, and our future."

Chris pauses intentionally. He wants the last statement about to resonate with the audience.

"In the United States we have the government infrastructure built to address the digital market. And it has not failed us in nearly eighty years. Why, because the founding standards of transparency, registration, regulation, and public disclosure that we built into our system that apply in the traditional securities sense, also apply to digital securities. Of course, like anything we have to adapt our framework to the changing times and technology, but the rules do not change. It's simple, corruption in all sectors, government, private and public sector is the root of all financial crimes, and now these financial crimes have found just another playground, virtual currency. And let's be clear, financial crimes hurt people. Often people focus on the word financial and think no one was harmed, and no one died. But the South African people are hurting because of this! Nguzo Saba also known as Bitcoin Investments on paper, was set up to provide a direct line of access to funds from donors to people in need of clean water. The Nguzo Saba virtual currency platform enabled directed donation giving, where they were able to skip all the costs that may be associated with bank transfers and currency exchange rates. The donations were done in Bitcoin. In exchange for the donations the company was supposed to build the clean water irrigation system and the donors would also receive utility tokens to use specifically on the platform. On the platform, the utility tokens could be used to pay for development types of services like to hire laborers to pave the street, electricians to install an electrical line, or builders to build a school. Thousands of dollars were donated, but the people in desperate need of water never received that water irrigation system. They do not have the clean water supply for basic necessities: to drink, to wash clothes, for their crops, to cook, for cleaning, and to survive. They struggle every day, but why and for what?!"

Chris pauses and takes a deep breath.

"We have to ask ourselves, where was the diligent monitoring and enforcement? Where were the registration, reporting, and disclosures? How could we allow a purported company to operate, and not know anything about its existence, who owned the company, who were their employees, where and how did they amass the money to operate the company, what was the companies function, what were their obligations to their investors, and how did they use their investor's money? These are the questions we must ask. And this is crucial because we cannot ignore the fact that there are communities that need access to the marketplace, and virtual currencies present a unique opportunity for inclusion of the unbanked populations to the marketplace. And our mandate helps them. We must regulate to reduce the risk posed to these populations, so that people will not suffer from a Nguzo Saba scheme again!

South Africa, you have the tools, you just have to use and enforce them. The United States believes South Africa can be our partner to lead in the fight to tackle fraud, manipulation, and corruption in virtual currencies. The United States will continue to stand with South Africa to foster genuine opportunity and inclusion in the fintech market. Thank you."

Clapping ensues as Chris walks off the stage. He shakes the hand of the Prime Minister and Financial Minister of South Africa, and other dignitaries and special guests.

Bitcoin can provide the most obvious benefit to the South African people, financial inclusiveness. Bitcoin and blockchain enable the unbanked population to have access to the market, and therefore, get paid. No longer did anyone need permission to open a bank account, maintain a minimum balance, or possess a certain credit score. No need to rely on a centralized institution, such as the government or a bank for permission to open a bank account. The only thing most people will need is a smartphone. The smartphone granted access to the world, and retailers are already accepting cryptocurrencies for goods and services.

It was not too long ago that Nguzo Saba captured international news and rocked the country. There were protests demanding investigations and prosecutions, but the government continued to be tight lipped about everything. Many people thought, that there would be riots, but the people were really upset at the government. How could anyone blame them? In their eyes, minds, and hearts, the government allowed Nguzo Saba to steal their money.

A lot was said, but it was everything that was not said that was telling. The South African government's silence was at the SEC's direction. The SEC and the FBI investigation into the Locke Market website had traced some of the cryptocurrency for the opioid drug trafficking scheme right back to Nguzo Saba. But that conversation was for tomorrow morning. Now was the time to be diplomatic.

* * *

Back in the United States, Mitch is freaking out.

Just how much did the Chairman know? What did the full Locke report say and had the Chairman read it? Mitch did not have the security clearance to have access to the full report. Mitch only knew what he had been privy to in staff meetings and basically what was leaked to the media. He had tried to get information discreetly through colleagues and drinking buddies over at the FBI but had not obtained much.

And what did the South African industry officials know about him and how they were all linked to Nguzo Saba? How could he be so stupid, and so careless? He thought. He could see the media headlines now, "Right under the SEC Chairman's nose, SEC assistant with potential gave it all up to be a drug trafficker."

And where the fuck is Mike? Mitch thought. He was supposed to be here ten minutes ago.

"This is all Mike's fucking fault. This is what I get for just trying to help a friend," Mitch said out loud.

Replaying the acts in his head that led him to this position, Mitch sits down. His leg bounces up and down and thinks to himself.

I just wanted to make a few more bucks. I was doing pretty well earning Bitcoin by mining it, but I wanted something to call my own. When Mike came to me with this great idea to start our own cryptocurrency, I jumped at it.

I had the computer programming skills to build our own platform. It was quite simple by beginning with the public source code, which I improved to do what we wanted. But I really didn't know how to run a business. That was Mike's arena. I kind of allowed him to take full reign without question. I should've known better, but I trusted him. He was responsible.

In some ways he took advantage of me. The platform was growing exponentially, and our currency value was skyrocketing. And all I saw was the glitz of success. I didn't double check the numbers. I didn't know everyone who was working our company, namely in South Africa under the auspices of business development consultants. My signature was used to open bank accounts in Columbia, Panama, Sweden, where funds were diverted from Nguzo Saba.

I signed off on documents that I did not read and did not care to read. I would just ask Mike what it was, and he would tell me it was for investments to diversify the company stock portfolio or something mundane and standard like state licensing paperwork. Usually Mike would approach when I was knee deep in computer coding. Not even able to take my eyes off the computer screen, I would just scribble my name where there was an "X" mark.

Mitch scolded himself aloud, "How could I have been so stupid!?"

There is a knock at the door. Mitch looks through the peep hole. It's Mike.

Without answering or saying a word, Mitch slips a note under the door. The computer typed note instructs Mike to get back in his car, drive home, walk to the nearest train station and order a taxi back to the house and come in through the basement door.

The knocking stops.

Mitch goes downstairs to the basement, unlocks the door and waits.

Ninety minutes later the basement door swings open.

"Finally, hurry up inside." Mitch said slightly alarmed.

"What the hell was that all about with the door?!" Mike asks.

"We have to be careful. People may be watching and listening. Where have you been Mike?!" Mitch asked with a look of disgust.

"I had to get some things together," Mike replies, struggling inside the house with a suitcase.

"Shhh. Lower your voice, you know I have roommates. Follow me to the laundry room." Mitch says.

Mitch turns on the washing machine and adds an extra twenty minutes to the rinse cycle to start.

"Go ahead. Now you can talk." Mitch states.

"I went to speak with a lawyer," said Mike.

Mitch's eyes widen with panic, "What did you say?"

"I told her everything Mitch."

"Everything, like what? Mike?"

"I told her about what we did. The company, the investments, the money that went missing, everything and she advised me…" Mike answers.

"What we did?" Mitch interjects. Mitch's balled fist bangs on top of the washer. "We did not do anything." Mitch points at Mike. "You did this. You and Jones did this, not me. You need to find where that money is and give it back." Mitch's eyebrows squint together.

"The money is gone; Jones took it all. I don't know where he is at or where he is hiding the money. What are we going to do?" Mike asks.

We? Mitch thought.

There was only but so many ways this could turn out. Jail, public humiliation and shame, or going into hiding and living as a fugitive. Neither is an option for Mitch. He is not made for jail and he cannot save face in front of any congressional inquiry. And what is a life you cannot live.

"How is it just gone? All gone. How?" Mitch asks.

"You and I were not supposed to get cut out. I got assurances from Jones that we would be good. Take a little off the top just to pay some bills, little things. But Jones has taken off and I cannot get in touch with him." Mike answers.

Mitch grabs Mike up by the shirt, holding Mike against the wall. "Where is my money, Mike? How could he just take money that is supposed to be invested? You helped him! I know you did! Say it! Admit it!"

Mike is struggling to get Mitch off him. Kicking he yells, "Get the fuck off me. Get the fuck off!" Mike manages to throw a punch but Mitch's grip on him tightens.

"Come on! Why would I be here if I set you up?! Why?! I'm not stupid, and it would be stupid for me to steal from you and come all the way down here. I would be long and gone if I had!" Mike yells.

Mitch responds, "Only because you had no choice. He double crossed you and stole from you too! That's why you're here! You don't care about me! I just bought a house with a mortgage I clearly don't have money for and took out a loan for the $75,000 I gave him."

Mike is breathing heavy. "No, it's not like that! We promised 7% and we had to deliver. We take a little off the top from one investor to pay another investor. We were seeing our investment grow so much; it was nothing to do. This was just easier to do them to try pay out each investor individually from their specific investment growth. And Jones said no paperwork just moving the original investment around as paid by check or bank transfer. It was already liquid unlike the Bitcoin. It was quick, so we did that to get back to our lives."

Mitch sucks teeth, "to your endless partying and drinking, right?"

Mike does not answer him, and Mitch let's go of him.

"Where is Jones?" Mitch asks Mike again.

"I don't know. You guys should be closing in on him. There is a warrant out for his arrest, right? He is wanted for questioning in a SEC criminal investigation." Mike replies.

"You should have never got me involved. Don't go anywhere Mike. We are going down to the investment firm office now!"

Mike did not want to go but he got in the car anyway. He knew there was no office. He and Jones had rented the office for a week. They got some office furniture from a business that was closing, and Bitcoin Investments LLC was born. Mike had brought Mitch by the office when he first sought Mitch's investment. They sat down, had coffee, tea, and bottled water waiting for him. A couple of shiny objects distracted him from questioning anything. All Mitch saw, and that was the intent, was the investment name practically in lights. In gold coloring on the office door, stationary paper, office building directory, a couple pens and some mail, mostly business magazine subscriptions. These things were relatively easy to get. The fake workers were a little more difficult to get, but Jones resorted to blackmail and bribery of family, friends, former associates, and even strangers.

These things were also easy to dispose of. Mitch realized this and more when there was a "for rent" sign on the front door of what was Bitcoin Investment LLC. There was no company name on the door.

Mitch went down the steps, heading to the leasing office. At the receptionist desk, Mitch asks, "Is Frank in?"

"Frank?" The receptionist asks.

"Yeah," he responds.

"There is no one by that name that works here," the receptionist states.

"No. I need to speak with him now." Mitch says.

"Sir, there is no Frank. Can I help you with anything else?" The receptionist asks.

"No there is a Frank, I met him. Matter of fact, I had coffee with him in the back office. I walked right through here." Mitch states and begins to walk to the back of the leasing office.

"Sir you can't go back there!" the receptionist states.

"I walked right by a cactus. Yes, I see it is right there." Mitch responds pointing.

"Sir, I am going to have to call police if you keep going. Come with me. Security is already on its way." the receptionist states.

"Okay. Okay. Maybe you can help me." Mitch responds.

The receptionist looks at Mitch. Mitch sits down in the chairs in the waiting area and asks, "Perhaps the owner of the business Bitcoin Investments LLC, they were leasing the fourth-floor unit left a forwarding address for his mail or contact if any issues?" Mitch asks.

"Are you sure you're in the right place. No one is renting the fourth-floor unit. It has been vacant forever. If you know someone interested in the space, please let me know." She smiles at Mitch.

"Mr. Jones has the fourth-floor unit for his company, Bitcoin Investments. You know Mr. Jones?" Mitch begins to panic. "You got to know him."

"Sir, you okay, are you feeling okay?" The receptionist asks Mitch. "Would you like some water?"

But Mitch plunges ahead and asks the receptionist, "Do you have any paperwork on Mr. Jones for the rent of the fourth-floor unit upstairs?"

"I'm sure we have no paperwork for a Mr. Jones."

"Miss, can you just check. Please."

She nods. Opens the file drawer, sifts her hand on top of the folders tab names then closes the drawer.

Mitch gets up. "Maybe look again." Mitch is peering over the receptionist desk, looking at the drawer.

"I did sir. It's not in there. I am checking our computer system now to see if anything exists, where it might be." The receptionist responds.

"I was here a few months ago with Frank and Mr. Jones, right here talking to them."

"Was the unit rental temporary or long term?" The receptionist asks.

"I don't know." Mitch replies.

She opens another cabinet drawer and begins to flick through the folder labels. Mitch is looking too, watching her look through the drawer. She closes the drawer. "Sir there is nothing here. I wish I could have been more help. Sorry."

Mitch storms out of the leasing office by Mike, back up the steps to the fourth-floor unit. Mike is right behind him. Mitch checks the doorknob to see if the door is unlocked. It is and he turns the knob, opens the door fully, and walks in. Peering around, nothing, just empty. You would never be able to tell that people worked here, that a company existed.

"We are never going to find him. Jones is probably not even his real name." said Mike.

"You stole money from people with Jones, money you never intended to give back. And now you are surprised? I can't believe you." Mitch responds.

Mitch is standing in the middle of an empty office, carpet torn, surrounded by white walls.

"What are you going to tell Mr. Richards? He gave you his savings, part of retirement for you to invest too. He practically raised you, and you are all he has. People I know trusted me, trusted you. And you just handed them over to Jones like a mark." he said to Mike.

"A few hundred here, a thousand there, nothing big. It didn't matter, we were set to make millions," Mike mused.

"There were never even investments or stock trades taking place? He was just keeping the money for himself." Mitch states.

"Mike, you must know some people that can get their hands on some money. They can help you out, and you can get the money back to them in a few months." Mitch tells Mike.

Mike just looks at Mitch. He doesn't say a word.

"So, you're not going to tell me? Should I be worried about South Africa?" Mitch asks Mike.

"Mitch, I thought you knew people in some pretty high places, working for the government and all. And I cannot be a part of this," Mike said.

"But you can solve this. Pick up the phone and make a few phone calls. You know exactly who to call. They will protect us, at least for a little while, which is all we need to figure things out. After all, we cannot have this kind of blow-back on the SEC Chairman, now can we?" Mike tells Mitch.

"I cannot get my work involved or anyone that may have a potential connection. They're going to want something in return or better yet a blanket check to cash in for a favor at any time. Just blackmail the rest of my career. No. Not going to do it." Mitch answers.

"Mitch, this is politics man. I mean you signed up for this. Whether now or later, something was bound to happen, and you were bound to call on the D.C. elite to help." Mike states.

Mitch makes the call.

CHAPTER 11

BLACK AND WHITE

The reality is that the Nguzo Saba scheme was only one of many misuses of Bitcoin. There are tumblers and mixers on the cryptocurrency exchange that are set up to prevent law enforcement from knowing who made exchanges. This is a hurdle to CFTC enforcement investigations. The CFTC assigned most of their investigators to work around the clock on the scheme. But the scheme was the first to be investigated and documented, with some actual resources behind it. Once there was an alleged connection to money laundering and the Department of Justice wanting to claim a win, use of all resources at their disposal was justified. There was even now a task force assigned and the task force's first meeting was about to begin.

"Good morning all. I know it's early, but we want to get started with new assignments and top priorities as soon as possible. Those at the top believe a lot of time has been wasted and we cannot have that. There are also concerns of people keeping information to themselves, not reporting to their superiors. That ends now." He motions to the staff standing behind the table to close the conference door. "I want you now to give your attention to Joe, whom has been one of the investigators leading the investigation since the beginning. Joe."

Joe stands. "Here's what we know so far. About a year ago, there was an ICO launch in South Africa. A few months after that there was an ICO launch here in California, Bitcoin Investments." Joe hits the board with his paper. "What we didn't realize at the time but know now is that the ICO white papers was virtually identical. At first not much thought was put into it because the language used in these papers are usually the same. But the spelling of certain words reflected the South African English accent. From there, we took a closer look, and dug a little deeper. Finding that South African government leaders were potentially investors in the start-up of this ICO or involved somehow exerting at least some influence. The ICO in California went forward, and some complaints by small investors that after investing, there were issues with their financial transactions, but nothing significant to raise any flags."

Walking to the other side of the board, Joe continues. "Twelve weeks ago, was the timeline set for when the token should have been complete and introduced into the market but nothing, investors have not heard anything, and it is following a pattern. In South Africa, their citizens were not just promised a return on their investment but also that profit over twenty-five percent of interest made on the investment would go toward environmental infrastructure. On the board you also see both the South African and California ICO are linked to this company, Nguzo Saba. We have some stuff. But we need to know all the players in California and how they are connected or got connected to the players in South Africa and the United States." Joe is pointing to papers on the board. "How the fraud is being perpetrated and covered up here in America, and where American investors' money is going? We need you to speak with me about every credible lead you have and do follow-up on lead. We will chase down every lead if necessary, to put names on this board."

Joe's boss speaks. "Okay, any questions for Joe?" Silence. "Okay. I expect everyone to follow-up with Joe on those leads. We can continue with meeting any other updates from the task force."

"I know the SEC Chairman met with some South African officials in his recent visit. I don't know if the meeting was formal or informal, but it was a topic of discussion, especially in light of his comments on Nguzo Saba. Our intel tells us he met with them in private and his assistant was not there. Something confidential was discussed that he didn't want anyone to have privy to but him, and the meeting was not on his itinerary schedule," said the task force agency liaison.

"Find out everything you can on that meeting. Poke around. See what our little friends at the SEC know. See what spills out." Joe's boss responds.

A CFTC investigator asks, "What is going on at Department of Justice? What do they have on this?"

"You know everybody is quiet. But I believe their using traditional tactics at their disposal now. Contacts they have in the region and international companies. You know corrupt politicians and companies tend to run in similar groups. I don't expect them to be charging anyone soon, as still investigating too."

Staff murmurs among each other in the room, "Alright, anything else?" The boss looks around, "Okay, back to work."

Phones are ringing. Coffee cups line the garbage cans on the right side of the desks all the way from the elevator to the large office file cabinets next to the boss's office. Across from Joe sits his colleague. They have shared this space, desk-to-desk for years. Between chews of his muffin the colleague states, "Joe, what's the plan?"

"There is a lead I got, a tip that the company used to lease an office downtown. Going to talk to some people, stop by the leasing office and ask some questions. Try to get some answers."

"Okay, I can come with."

"I got it." Joe gets up and grabs his coat off the back of his chair. He gets in the elevator and walks out of the office. Gets in his car and drives downtown. His car tells him that his wife is calling. He doesn't answer. "I'll call her back when I'm finished." His wife is calling him again. This time he answers.

"Hey. Is everything okay?" He asks his wife.

"Okay, you know that I'm working, can't really have this conversation now."

The light turns green. Joe looks to his left before hitting the gas.

"I know. I understand. I am doing my best. Can we talk about this when I get home?" Joe replies.

Joe breathes in. "I do come home. What are you talking about? You and the kids are important to me, and so is my job." Joe is waiting for a response, "Hello?!" Nothing, silence. "Janice?!" The phone call ends.

"Shit!" Joe makes a right on the main avenue turning into the office building of Bitcoin Investments. Joe parks his car and walks into the leasing office.

At the leasing office, Joe demands the lease records on Bitcoin Investments and information on all applications to lease property six months before and after their lease term ended. "You know you are the second person this month to come by and seek information on Bitcoin," said the leasing agent.

Joe replies, "Who?"

"I don't know. A couple guys, young, were acting paranoid. Like I told them, we don't have any information on a Bitcoin Investments. I don't remember that company leasing any office space here."

"Can you describe them for me?" Joe asks.

"Well early to mid-twenties, white men, got a…Wait, why you want to know? What's going on? Are they in some kind of trouble?" The receptionist asks.

"It's an ongoing investigation. Just answer my questions. They have any identifying marks or anything you noticed?" Joe asks.

"What is your name? Are you a cop? And let me see your badge?" The receptionist asks.

"I don't have time for this! Just tell me what day they came here and were…" Joe states.

"I know my rights! Either you show me your badge or you can leave!" leasing agent states pointing to the door. "Just like I told them other boys, there is no paperwork for a tenant by that name."

Joe responds, "I can come back here with a warrant and force you to hand over all your records. I don't want that for you. I don't think you want that either. But if you do not give me the records and information I requested, I won't have a choice. I'm sure there is bound to be something you do not want us snooping around and finding things that do not add up. I don't need to do that because that is not why I am here. What is it going to be?" Joe states.

"Are you threatening me?!" The receptionist asks.

"I am just making an observation and laying out the options you have." Joe states.

"I can't give you what I don't have. You can go ahead and get a warrant. Now this is my place of business and since you do not have a warrant, you can leave now! This is private property!" The receptionist states.

Joe chuckles. "I won't be going anywhere. I don't care what you think your rights are." He sits down in the chair in front of the leasing agent's desk. He puts his legs up on top of the desk, making himself comfortable.

"I'm calling my lawyer!" The receptionist yells.

"Sounds good, okay, I'll wait. While we are waiting, can I get some water or something? Maybe coffee if it's not too much trouble. We might be here a while." Joe states.

* * *

As soon as he dials the numbers, Mitch knows it's a mistake. Mitch is on the phone with the agency ethics hotline, an alleged anonymous service that allows employees to seek advice, file complaints, and/or report suspicious activity. Mitch is waiting on the phone to speak with someone, and the elevator music that was playing made him more anxious. The time waiting ultimately defeated him with his nerves winning out, as he played different scenarios and outcomes. A person finally came on the line "Hello, what can I…" Mitch hangs up. He decides to just speak with Chairman Chris Donaldson in person. That is the plan. Mitch finds himself at Chris's home later that night.

It was late, after 10:00 p.m. He knocks on the door. Chris answers, "Do you know what time it is? This better be an emergency." Mitch is shaking and responds, "I would not be here if it was not. May I come in?"

Chris opens the door fully and steps to the side to allow Mitch into his house. Mitch walks through the door. Chris locks the door, then turns back around to look at Mitch, and states "I was not expecting you. Is everything okay?"

Mitch looks him in the eye, "I would have called. But no, everything is not okay." Mitch spills it all. He tells Chris everything.

Chris states, "So you are saying he had no idea about any of this and Bitcoin Investments ties to Nguzo Saba?"

"Yes, I didn't know."

"And does this Mike involved in this Ponzi scheme have a last name?"

"I can't remember it right now. But I can show you a picture of him from his social media. That might be helpful in identifying him too, his real name probably not Mike either. He is probably going to try and skip town too." Mitch is on his phone, checking social media.

"Look here he is. This is him." Mitch states showing Chris a picture of Mike.

"Are you sure that's him?" Chris asks.

"Yes!" Mitch answers him.

"That's my nephew." Chris states.

"Yes, he is the one that introduced me to Bitcoin Investments and the owner and everything. Wait, wait, your nephew?!"

"So, you are just innocent in all this? That is what you expect me to believe?" Chris asks.

"I am saying that I did not knowingly participate or create this scheme. I lost my money. I was taken advantage of. Why would I scheme myself out of my money? That would make no sense. And I didn't know Mike is your nephew." Mitch responds.

"And you are coming to me with this, why?" Chris asks.

"I don't know what to do and I need help." Mitch answers.

"Mitch! This is an ongoing investigation that involves multiple agencies, and we are directly investigating. I do not know how you thought this would be appropriate to disclose to me. I will have to report it. This places the whole division and agency reputation and work in this case at risk now! Do you understand that!?" Chris states.

"Yes, but—"

Chris cuts Mitch off, "No buts! And where is Mike, why is he not answering his phone!?" Chris is dialing Mike's number again. "You call him and see if he answers." Chris directs Mitch. Mitch calls Mike but no answer.

"Here is what you are going to do. You are going to get in touch with Mike and tell him to bring his ass here. I am going to make a few calls. You are going to need a lawyer and PR to help you with your statement etc. They will help prep you, for what is about to come." Chris states.

"Chairman, what is going to happen to me?" Mitch asks.

"You are in the fight of your life. Your career is over, so forget about it. But maybe you can retain some respect, so that you can have some sort of life after." Chris looks at him. "You have to be strong. It's late. You need to stay here. You can sleep in the guest room."

Mitch follows Chris to the guest room. "Here are extra sheets and blankets if you need it. There is a remote for AC and heat if you need to adjust the temperature. Towels and toiletries are in the closet too. And the bathroom is across the hall on the left. I get up early on Saturdays, so I'll wake you up and we will talk further about this in the morning." Chris states.

"Okay." Mitch responds.

"See you in the morning." Chris leaves the room and closes the door behind him.

Mitch is not sleeping. He is wide awake, lying in the bed fully clothed with his shoes on staring at the ceiling. Thinking over and over what flags he missed. He calls Mike again, but there is no answer. "How could I be so stupid?" He whispered. "I shouldn't be here. Mike is his nephew. He's not going to believe me. He is going to choose his family over me. That is why Mike is so cavalier about all this. He is the nephew of the SEC Chairman, my boss. He is protected."

Mitch went through every single conversation he had with Mike about Bitcoin Investments. He pictures himself at the meeting in the office building downtown, trying to recall any detail that may lead to Jones' real identity, something that he missed telling the Chairman tonight. Mitch cannot sleep. All he can think about is tomorrow. He must prepare himself.

"I can't go to jail." He states to himself. "He said my career is over and I will have to fight for my life. But I did nothing wrong." Mitch gets up and paces from left to right. He mumbles, "Unfucking believable. This is some bullshit. What did I do to deserve this? This is not right." He sat on the bed and cried himself to sleep.

* * *

"In the beginning we did not want to rely upon the traditional financial power structure. But now the companies and innovations that Bitcoin spawned are now finding themselves in the same place as the dot com startups. Bitcoin has outgrown the original spirit of the company. Replaced by businessmen in fancy suits," said Moto.

Cryptocurrency in its purest form is not subject to SEC regulation because they are not securities. They may be a commodity and depending on the circumstances may be a property. But our innovation was no longer limited to any one form. There were now entities that would hold your crypto for safekeeping. These are called wallets. If you are interested in trading but need guidance, you may want to look up cryptocurrency trusts that engage in cryptocurrency trade. If you want to get some value out of your crypto in physical currency, this may be achieved through exchanges. Exchanges allow you to kind of cash out your cryptocurrency for the value rate of your crypto in Euro, Yen, and USD at that specific time.

Brad replies, "I know, and I understand Moto. But once you reach a certain size, you question the longevity of the original intent. You cannot have both principal and scalability. You want profit."

Moto states, "Profit was never supposed to be the driving factor behind every decision."

Brad responds, "You must have been kidding yourself to actually think that Bitcoin could operate outside of government regulation forever. With the market valued currently at $65 billion. You thought a billion-dollar market, where less than a year ago was as high as $500 billion was going to be overlooked. Even if that was Bitcoin's peak, it got the government's attention."

"That is not the point Brad!"

"I know where you are going with principles and all. No ties to the corporate financial structure. I know I get it. I was there in the beginning. We built this together." Brad states.

"But this is no longer realistic Moto, because this is a business. In order to be successful and ensure scalability, we had to bring in talent that knows how to run a business. This is why we invested in financial planning in the first place. This was all building up to this, the inevitable. Look at the proliferation from the original concept of cryptocurrencies that you had to now. So many variations and they all do something a little different. Digital currency typically serves as a medium of exchange, in comparison to tokens that usually serve as stores of value that allow purchase of a good or service on a particular platform. Crypto-assets that are securities where there is investment in platform in exchange or expectation of share of interest in platform or increase in value of investment upon return."

Moto grabs a glass from the wet bar and pours a glass of scotch. He takes a long gulp as he gazes out the window. Brad continues to talk as Moto falls into a daze. Everything looks so small from up here, Moto thought. Directly in his line of vision is the S&P billboard.

BC Trusts is operating in a grey area and had been for a long time. Not only regarding government regulation, but to what the future of the company would hold, and what did survival of the company look like. Moto feels as if he was the only one wrestling with the founding principles of Bitcoin and its purpose. What would sacrifice of these principles actually mean? Innovation would continue without them regardless. It was clear to Moto that Bitcoin belonged to the world now for them to do as they choose, even if it was not what he would do.

Bitcoin revolutionized the industry. And even if Moto did not know what the future held for Bitcoin, maybe it was necessary for the vision to change. They have achieved their purpose by all accounts. Bitcoin is now a global currency. People are using Bitcoin to innovate, create, and do more than ever before.

"Listen, Moto." Brad clears his throat.

"Hello?" Brad repeats himself.

"Do you hear me, Moto?"

Moto snapped out of his daze. "These regulated financial institutions collect information about their customers, which they often monetize by selling their customer data, so much for regulation. Who do these regulations actually protect? Investors, the institutions. Not customers, not the worker, not you and me."

"Who do you think you are Moto, the worker?" Brad chuckles. "We are an institution."

"Wall Street, the government, the banks, those are the institutions. That is who we are up against," Moto states.

"Listen, Brad, we have to push back, we will put up a legal and policy fight. We have contacts and friends, let's use them."

"Are you sure about this? We will have to inform the Board and shareholders." Brad asks.

"Yes! But I do have a call right now. We can schedule everything later. Please close my door on the way out," Moto states.

Moto ponders to himself. Just to think that in the beginning my friend just wanted to mine enough Bitcoin to buy a pizza or two a month. Now there was a new crypto on the market every day. The "internet of things." Moto continues to stare out the window down at all the bustle of people in the city. He could not exactly see them, but he knew them. Everyone always seemed in a rush, likely heading to work, running in and out of stranger cars, walking with a mouth full of food. And he knew everyone's hand was holding a cell phone, their eyes glued to the screen.

People watching, some may say it was rude or downright creepy. But it was America's favorite past time just like in personal communication.

Ding. Ding.

Moto just got a notification on his phone for something. Maybe an appointment reminder, more likely some social network app. He checks his phone. "Shit," he forgot about game night. Moto said, "Sam did not say anything. He probably forgot too. I am only going for Sam." He thought. Work took over their lives. Game night would be a much needed break. His mind needed a break. But Brad and Sean were bound to talk about work, at least a little. Maybe he should just go home. He had missed a bunch of game nights. Sam would not miss him. But there was no one at home, just a three-floor house full of furniture and expensive things, but no one. He'll just get a bottle of Jack and head over to Sam's.

"Good night," Moto says to the receptionist and presses the elevator button. It's almost the close of business, but his receptionist was still working. He briefly wondered why she was there, getting into the elevator, but he knew she would be there until he left no matter what time. In no time at all, Moto is at the parking level.

"Traffic is going to be crazy getting out of the valley." Moto speaks out loud to himself, "I have to stop and pick up the wine before I get on the highway." He gets in the silver mustang and drives down Jefferson. Traffic was light getting there and his organic mini supermarket is not crowded.

As he paces the aisles to the liquor section, Moto brushes by Mike.

Mike always stocks up on his favorite snacks before he starts working. Kola champagne, mozzarella sticks, microwaveable burger, energy shots, peanut chews, and Chico sticks. The last one was hard to come by. Mike finally finds the Chico sticks and heads to the front cashiers.

"Excuse me." Mike says. Moto turns his head and takes a step back. Mike grabs the energy shot and says, "Thank you." He gets back in line behind Moto.

Mike pedals down Jefferson about 3 miles before he crosses over the old trolley tracks in route home. There was a lot of construction. Luxury condos were being built like overnight. The crosswalks have fresh paint. There are no more potholes. Mike glides past a boy and a little girl standing on their porch. The grass is overgrown, windows bordered up with wood. Their fingers wrap around the handle of a suitcase. The moving van awaits them, right behind the SOLD sign.

Mike speeds around the corner. The bike chain ripples. He jumps the curb and coasts a few feet to the door. He jumps off his bike, book bag in tow, and goes up the stairs.

In the house, he pops the mozzarella sticks in the microwave, clearing the 7:00 p.m. time to heat up his food for three minutes. He heads straight to his computer, time to mine Bitcoin.

Bitcoin excites Mike.

Tap. Tap. Opens chips. *Crunch.*

Tap. Tap. Tap. Tap.

He strikes the keys so feverishly.

The microwave beeps, but he doesn't notice.

Beeping continues.

He sits there so focused on making the next Bitcoin.

Subconsciously, thoughts run through Mike's head. The most money I have ever made was through Bitcoin.

He must use the bathroom. He should not have drunk that soda. But he's almost there, seconds away from completing verification of the transaction. No breaks. There is no time for that.

The clock above Mike's head, a gift from his aunt, strikes 11:00 p.m.

He needs better software. Already two updated versions of the Bitcoin mining software had come out. Mike's software was two years old. Old software on a four-year-old computer didn't help. For most people four years is nothing. Most would pride themselves on making good use of one's money and taking care of their possessions, not wasting money on frivolous things not needed when you had a perfectly functioning computer. But what is functioning is subjective, as well as what is needed.

Mike is still going. Keys clicks, the sound of his hardware overheating is clear. It sounds like a microwave, but Mike must keep going.

He needs better everything. The curtains on his window are dingy and worn. He found his computer table outside by the trash dumpster.

But he does not have the money, at least not in physical form. He has some crypto and saves his money to pay the electricity bill.

He wipes his eyes. Takes a swig of the last of his energy shot with his left hand, pops candy in his mouth with his right hand, and then he is back at it.

He taps the keys.

Almost there.

Mike is competing with hundreds if not thousands of people across the world, some with better equipment then him, more skills, but he did not care he was determined to win. This was his normal schedule.

"Come on! Come on! Come on! Damn!"

Another miner verified the transaction, beating him and earning a few Bitcoins.

Mike sucks his teeth, flings headphones off his ears and goes to the kitchen for a snack. He has frozen pizza that would cook quickly in the microwave. He opens the microwave and seeks the mozzarella sticks. They look hard. Substituting the mozzarella sticks for the pizza, he places the pizza on the plate and bites into the mozzarella stick while he waits. Snacking, the mozzarella stick is cold, and the cheese filling is not the way it is supposed to be. No cheese dangling from the bite, just one bite and the cheese is gone. Mike chews the whole cold cheese filling like a cheese stick. The last bite of the mozzarella stick is all breading. He continues to eat the mozzarella sticks, his back leaning against the kitchen top, right foot crossed in front of the left.

The microwave beeps and the pizza's finally ready. He can smell it. Making his way back to the computer, he plops down in front of the screen. He takes a couple bites of the pizza and chews. He holds the remaining portion of the pizza in his mouth. Wipes his hands on his jeans then begins to mine again.

He takes his hands off the keyboard every so often to bite his pizza. He chomps, staring at the screen ever so intently. The screen is so bright.

Keys tapping, the computer is working overtime.

Taking a break from chewing, Mike pulls open the drawer on his computer table and pulls out his headphones. He would usually play his music out loud, but he already had the neighbors complain twice this week, and the last time they subtly threatened to call the police on him.

Party techno beats are playing through his ears. He is moving his head in rhythm; shoulders follow and feet moving to the beat. He is jamming as he mines well into the next day. Daily, he worked away on his computer while most slept.

But the people were up working: the single parent, working black man and woman, immigrant, and working poor, whom often held more than one job and had been predetermined to live a life of paycheck-to-paycheck and/or physical labor, but decided their own destiny.

Mike's cell lights up. Mitch is calling him, but he does not answer. This called is followed by a call from Uncle Chris.

Keys tapping.

Still typing, Mike cracks his neck.

"Yes, that is what I'm talking about!"

He stretches his arms, yawns, and a grin emerges across his face.

Two Bitcoins pour into Mike's Bitcoin account.

His uncle Chris is calling him again. He misses the call.

Mike starts at it again. The cycle continues for hours.

Around 8:00 a.m., Mitch calls him again, but it rings until it goes to voicemail. Phone is lighting up with notifications. "I really got to turn off notifications from the group chat. They really must be doing too much. They must not have a job or a life." Mike states.

Mike's inner thoughts fill his mind again while he works.

Mike does not have a boss telling him what to do, how to do it, and for how long. He makes his own schedule; he can work from the comfort of his own home and does not need experience. It made no sense to him that prospective employers hiring for entry level positions wanted experience. They say they want to pay a fresh out of college student wage and only require a bachelor's degree but require two to three years of substantive work experience. On what planet would he have that experience and if he does not get a chance, then how can he gain experience?

Mike jumps up and makes a dash to the toilet. He lifts the seat. He has held it for too long, and sighs relief. A few seconds more and he probably would not have made it to the bathroom. He runs his hands under the sink water. Wipe his hands on his jeans as he exits the bathroom.

Back at the computer, mining, internal grumbling resumes.

Keys tapping.

Mike's Bitcoin account is now tallied at 5,764 Bitcoins, an increase of 15 Bitcoins since he started mining. His total coins were valued at a little over $50,000. Mike looks up at the clock.

"Shit! It's 5:00 p.m.!" Nearly twenty-four hours had flown by.

He pulls himself out of his chair. He looks for his phone. Throwing clothes off his loveseat, he searches between the cushions.

His stomach grumbles more pronounced now. He walks to his kitchenette and spots his phone on top of the microwave, on top of his train ticket, one-way outbound departure from San Fran. The screen shows eight missed calls and forty-five unread messages. He unlocks the phone to see who has called and texted him. Mitch and his Uncle Chris were calling him all day.

Mike walks less than three feet to his bathroom shower. He is going to be late for the monthly family dinner at his Aunt's house. He didn't want to raise suspicion. He is close to making enough Bitcoin to hold him over for about a year but is not there yet. It will have to be enough. He packs his suitcase.

CHAPTER 12

PANIC ATTACK

———

Somewhere it all went left. Bitcoin was simply supposed to be a medium of exchange, a store of value, but with development emerged digital economies, solely operated for the purpose of amassing the value of the set cryptocurrency at play. But this was foretold. Bitcoin had made its public debut as a commodity for exchange on the futures trading market in 2015 and by 2017, Bitcoin was literally digital gold.

They wanted to play with the big boys, and they wanted to compete with Wall Street. Bitcoin went public on the crypto stock market. No one could have guessed that one Bitcoin would be valued at $20,000. And life was good.

Moto, Sam, Sean, and Brad are in the conference room of the company office toasting with champagne. It may only be 2:00 p.m. on a Wednesday, but this was a time for celebration.

Sean raises his glass. "Here's to us."

Moto clicks his glass with Sam, "To Bitcoin!"

"We did it, I could never have imagined. This is crazy and amazing bro!" Sam exclaims.

Brad is ecstatic too. He would finally be able to get his dream home. Maybe even quit his job and focus on the business full time. Not have to worry when retirement came. He can do this in retirement from the law. Bitcoin had already set him up to be able to have enough savings to put his god children through college.

Sean makes a grand gesture, "This is not the end of the celebration. We are going to kick things off right." He presents them each with a square jewelry box case."

They open the boxes and snugged in the velvet cushion are keys.

"These are keys to what?" Sam asks jingling the keys.

"Well, you guys are going to have to see for yourself. Get your stuff, we are taking the rest of the day off and heading to the pier."

"It's a helicopter." Sam asserts, grabbing his things.

"No, it's got to be a boat. I'm telling you guys, a yacht. I can see it now." Brad says.

Moto states, "I'm going to meet you guys downstairs, I got to make a quick phone call." He walks out of the conference room. Sean watches Moto through the glass, walking down the hall toward his office.

Sean goes to Moto's office and peeks his head into his office room.

Knock. Knock.

Moto looks up. "Yes, what up?"

The rest of Sean's body becomes visible as he enters. He closes the door. "A phone call Moto, really? What's going on?"

"All this is unnecessary, and you know it. I thought you were different."

"What? Have you never heard that a happy staff and work environment make a more productive team and company?"

"Are you unhappy here, Sean."

"No, of course not."

"So then don't spew that bullshit to me. You know better than to try and game me, Sean."

"What do you want from me, Moto? Everyone likes nice things, new things. We got to enjoy life and our hard work. Why not celebrate?"

"This is what it's all about for you, isn't it? It always has been. Just so clear to me right now that you are not supportive of the agenda. We need to reinvest, not waste money on things we don't need. That boat, airplane, depreciates half in value, the moment it is taken off the lot. We need more and stronger infrastructure. We need to spend more money on research. We can discover what other areas of the industry we can change. We need to tap talent, people with creative ideas who live across the world. And we need to compensate them well, more than just the bare minimum 'living' wage. Bitcoin is a steppingstone. If we continue to build on our reputation, we can really do things in this world. Beyond a fucking yacht, which I don't fucking need."

"Whoa, Moto, you just need to relax and enjoy life. Take a vacation or something."

Sean opens the office door and pauses, "You should know that you don't have to fix the world. You are only one human being. Don't carry that burden."

Moto turns from his laptop to face Sean. "Spending money with no purpose is just wasteful. It's not going to make you happy or fill that void in yourself, which is even more of a shame because the money could have been used for something great."

Bitcoin's recent rapid climb on the crypto stock market was primarily thanks to the finance technology, "FinTech" industry. They were so intrigued by the prospects of making technology work for them. Some were skeptic as they were so deeply intertwined with the banks themselves to the extent that they could not act, could not make decisions without a nod of approval from the banks. Some were literally institutions themselves masked as technology innovation divisions.

They had a separate agenda too. They posited that in order to continue to grow, crypto would need retail and institutional buy-in. What they meant is that they needed buy-in from banks and that they would bring the investments to the table. They said without them, the crypto would never stabilize and because of that there would be no substantial investments for growth as crypto was deemed too risky.

In sum, the banks wanted a seat at our table, but they missed the memo. Crypto did not want the banks. The mortgage crisis and the Wall Street financial crisis caused and backed by banks, all who took risks. What they really were saying is that they were the only ones allowed to make risky decisions about your own money, no one else. What made the banks more qualified to make these decisions, many may say their expertise as this is the field they work in and they have the knowledge. But if you really think about it, they help to withhold that knowledge from the public. These so called "white papers" and risk assessments are either vague or using terminology that many cannot understand. This is intentional. They have an interest in keeping the knowledge to themselves so that you feel you need them. Banks may have their place, but not in crypto.

* * *

Moto wakes up around 6:00 a.m. It was Wednesday and traffic would be bad in San Fran just like every other day. Time to begin the daily regimen, he slaps cool water on his face. Heads downstairs to the kitchen, grabs the protein mix and puts two spoons in the blender with sixteen ounces of water. Moto is out the door for his morning run. He is back in no time and jumps in the shower. It is 7:45 a.m. when he gets out the shower, towel wrapped around his waist.

Moto gets dressed and is out the door. He gets in the car and is driving with one hand while he eats his breakfast (a banana) with the other. Driving was surprisingly smooth. He fiddled with the satellite radio station favorites to get his daily morning dose of the financial forecasts.

The usual babble permeates the car, analysts arguing about the Dow and so on.

"I don't expect too much movement today. We will likely see an increase in oil and crypto. But that has remained steady for some time. Wait, I'm hearing new developments. We are getting reports that Bitcoin stock value is taking a decline."

Analysts go back and forth on their opinions of Bitcoin.

"Bitcoin has been doing remarkable. But has it reached its peak?"

"You know this is the market. You got to take great risk to get great reward. A little decline is nothing. Those who bought in a few years ago when Bitcoin first came on the scene are walking away with profit anyway."

Other analyst interrupts.

Moto speaks out loud with a chuckle. "This should be good; you got an opinion too."

"Or maybe the market is responding to what this is, "the bubble effect." It was shiny and new, so everyone wanted it. But now with the influx of other crypto on the market, the unique value has dissipated."

Moto talks back to the radio, "Oh please. You don't know anything." He smocks.

Other analyst piggy backs on the last statement, "The elephant in the room has always been, does Bitcoin have sustainability? I think no. I know I don't want to invest in some random nobody who created this in his basement and got lucky. No experience. You just cannot trust it."

"Update! Bitcoin is tanking!"

That jolts Moto's attention. He speeds up in the lane. He must get to the office quickly, swerving in lanes and in and out of traffic, around carpool lanes.

"Come onnnnn!" Moto is rattling his fingers on the steering wheel as he grips it harder. "Where is the exit?!"

Honk. Moto presses down. *Hooooonnnnnkkkkk.*

"Come on drive or get out the way!"

Sadly, gossip about bank interest was a factor in Bitcoin's stock value increase. But what goes up must come down, and it crashed. Anyone who even earned 1 coin in the 2011 original launch of Bitcoin was looking to cash in now.

Panic ensued.

Every line was lit red, the phones ringing off the hook. The receptionist, all the assistants and the support staff were hands on deck. They were scribbling notes faster than their mouths could move.

"Thank you for calling Bitcoin, how may I direct your call," the assistant answered softly.

"I understand sir. At this time, the Board and Executive Leadership are hard at work…yes, we are sympathetic to what you are going through…sir, do not raise your voice at me. Please let me finish speaking. Here at Bitcoin, we are doing everything possible to figure out how and why this happened to our valuable customers like you."

The receptionist goes silent, likely tuning out the person ranting on the phone. She puts her hand over the phone and massages her temples as if she feels a headache coming. "Yes, I'm here sir, I'm listening." Her left hand is on her hip as she cradled the phone in her right hand.

"Unfortunately, no one is available at the time that can give you a concrete answer to your questions. But I can tell you that you should receive an email detailing if there are any next steps and status on the investigation. I can also take a message if you like."

The Bitcoin execs were in fact meeting and discussing next steps on how to assure customers and regain the trust from the market again, Moto, Sam, and Brad, everyone but Sean. He did not come in the office today and was not answering anyone's phone calls.

Bitcoin is being sold for less than six percent of its worth as value yesterday, and less than two percent of its worth as valued in the market last week. And Sean was missing in action.

"Have you heard from Sean?" Moto asked the receptionist. "No sir." Moto mumbled, "Typical."

"Excuse me, sir. I know this may not be a good time. But it's almost close of business. What do you want me to do about phones?" Cynthia asks Moto.

Moto tells Cynthia, "Just forward all calls automatically to voicemail. And please put in a request for help from temp staffing agency before you go. We are going to need more people to answer these phones. And Cynthia, thank you."

Moto makes his way back through the glass door of the waiting area to the offices. He slams his office door.

Moto starts pulling papers and supplies out of drawers. He takes piles of books from the shelves and stakes the books on his desk. He is pulling open cabinets, unhooking frames from the wall. Moto calls for his receptionist. "Hey, Cynthia I'm going to need a couple of file boxes. Thank you." Moto looks through the glass windows while he waits. He cannot really think with the phones ringing. But he wants to start something fresh and new on his own. He longs to feel free again.

Knock. Knock.

"Come in." Moto said. His receptionist walks in. "Here you go. Let me know if you need anything else." She states. "Thank you."

"Also, the temp agency will be sending over a dozen people tomorrow to answer phones. I am leaving now." Cynthia says. She stops short of leaving his office and turns around to Moto, "Should I come in tomorrow sir? Do I even have a job? Am I going to get paid?" Cynthia asks Moto.

"You will get paid. But this is not a good place for you. Protect yourself." Moto tells her.

Cynthia asks Moto, "Why?" Moto replies, "Because greed and selfishness corrupt good things and even good people. And they take everything around them down with them."

Moto grabs a file box and throws a few things into the box, his laptop, the blockchain white paper, and a signed copy of BC Trusts dissolution papers, removing him as a silent partner. He looks back at the stuff piled on chairs, the desk, and floor. "I don't need any of it." Moto says aloud. With his office packing complete, Moto walks to Sean's office. He places the original of the BC Trusts dissolution papers in the middle of Sean's desk. Moto picks up his file box and exits through the glass doors of BC Trusts for the last time and he never looks back.

* * *

Mitch takes off his watch and belt. He fumbles through his pockets for anything then places his suit jacket in the tray.

The SEC Chairman, Chris, is waiting for him on the other side. He walks behind him. No whispers, just stares, the sound of shoes follow the Chairman through the halls of Dirksen Senate Office building. The all white marble seems endless, just like the endless stream of suits standing on top of them. All day interest groups lobby these halls, one meeting after the other. They looked nice. And if you could look past the tailored suits and prepared talking points from years of grooming, you would see that there was no feeling behind those smiles. Not even belief in the actual system of government. They understood that as a human, anyone could be prodded to do what they wanted with the right incentive or at the right price. A few groups were desperately trying to help, advocating for communities traditionally ignored or silenced. But they were often out gunned by the resources, time, numbers, money of the interest groups, and ultimately the self-interest of the politician who occupied the office. One way or another democracy was losing.

The door opens. The Chairman and Ranking Member of the U.S. Committee on Banking, Housing and Urban Affairs enter. Everyone stands. The Chairman wastes no time, slamming today's issue of the Washington Times on the table.

Their staff had briefed them all day. The Chairman and Ranking Member for the last twenty-four hours have been pouring over memos that proffered to summarize the current state of law and the facts surrounding the fall of the crypto market. But what these memos really did was push a particular agenda. The arguments were persuasive because they were designed to come to a set conclusion.

"Read that." The committee chairman states.

Chris looks at the newspaper in silence.

"Indulge me Chris." The committee chairman states.

"Is this why I was summoned here?"

"Look I'm being asked a lot of questions, Chris. There has already been talk about setting up a new committee. If this gets away from us, then we may not be there to assist."

"Oh, the rumors."

"People want action, my constituents want action. My phone has been going off the hook nonstop since yesterday," the ranking member states.

"We have been on this all day. And we are using every resource at our disposal to gather all the facts so that we can take appropriate action. Figure out what went wrong... We cannot just be reactionary and make decisions off emotion."

"Oh, so you think that this man, Andrew, father of four, just walks into oncoming traffic following his loss of his savings in this cryptocurrency is emotion." The ranking member opens the first folder stacked on the table. "And another in Georgia."

The Committee Chairman pulls out another article from the folder. "Ohio. The district courts are reporting an uptake in phone calls seeking information on filing for bankruptcy. We have to get a handle on this, make the public rest assured in the government, or this can spiral out into a crisis."

Chris responds. "We have no way of knowing that the fall in crypto is the cause. We have to get the facts first."

"You think it's just a coincidence. That is not going to be enough for the American people!" The Committee Chair states.

"Are you planning legislation? Because if you are, we can schedule a briefing, memo, report, whatever you need on how and why the agency authorities can be changed." Chris turns to Mitch. "Are you getting this down?" Mitch shakes head in response.

"No notes! This meeting is not an official meeting, off the record." The committee chairman states. Looking at Mitch, he points, "You should go to lunch. We have quite a nice cafeteria in the basement."

Mitch looks at Chris. Chris's eyes connect with his approval. Mitch stands up and exits the room.

The committee chairman resumes. "The House is considering language for legislation now. The proposed legislation will target unfair or deceptive practices relating to transactions involving digital tokens. We are taking this issue seriously, as this is beyond just this incident, and with thinking ahead, we are recommending $25 million to be appropriated to the Federal Trade Commission to address this how they see fit."

"And how about us?" Chris asks.

"We think at this time, it is more appropriate for the SEC to redirect current funds as necessary." The ranking member answers.

"Excuse me!" Chris states.

"The legislation exempts digital tokens, like Bitcoin from being defined as securities, and even other proposals exempt non-financial businesses using blockchain from being defined as money transmitters. But we need to focus on the task at hand, this investigation," states the ranking member.

"You can't be serious? You care cutting our jurisdiction?" Chris asks.

"Do you guys even know what you are doing over there?" the committee chair asks.

"What can you tell us?" the Ranking Member follows up.

Chris answers. "We believe a big whale, someone with ownership of a large amount of Bitcoin, valued at hundreds of thousands at minimum sold all their Bitcoin, then flushed it back into the market, buying them back at a cheaper price and making millions. Creating panic and increasing instability until Bitcoin ultimately started plummeting. That is all we can share for now, still an ongoing investigation."

"You cannot be serious; you need to tell us everything you know." states the Committee Chair.

"Look, what we know for certain is that Bitcoin was trading on the market like usual, slight dips with value rises, like usual in any market, where trades make value go up or make value go down. Somehow, Bitcoin's value fell by tens of thousands in minutes. Some say it's due to geopolitical climate, others say look to the uncertainty in market analyst predictions." States Chris.

The Ranking Member follows up, "And what else?"

Chris responds. "We don't believe it's a lone actor, as would take significant amount of Bitcoin, so there is likely coordination among a group, they had to work together. Money looks like the motive, but we can never rule out some type of political or anti-government motivation."

"Basically, you don't know nothing, just a bunch of maybes and hypotheticals. That is what you're telling me." The ranking member responds.

Chris responds to the Ranking Member, "With all due respect. You don't even know what you are doing you are wasting time on a bill that is not going anywhere, it's just going to sit in a committee. When is the last time anything substantive was passed in Congress? Right now, that is a good thing. We are the experts in this arena, so please let us do our job!"

Shouting may have been expected. But silence fills the room. The committee chairman and ranking member are staring at Chris. They exchange glances among themselves. One by one, they slowly get out of their seats and exit the room. Only outside the room for less than fifteen minutes, Mitch had been trying to listen in, and he is slightly startled by the door swinging open with the Ranking Member and Committee Chair walking through right after the other. Mitch peered in the room and saw Chris coming out. Waiting there, Mitch saw the Committee Chair's staffers rushing toward them.

"I'm glad I caught you before you left Chris." She gasps and takes a breath. "You will receive a formal request in the morning. This is just a professional courtesy. The Committee will be calling you to testify before Congress."

* * *

Meanwhile at the SEC, Chris is rocking in his office chair, pondering what are we going to do? What do we say to the public, to the media?

Now everyone was looking to the government for answers, and someone to blame. Namely, Chris, he was in charge of the agency that's supposed to prevent this. But he did not have the answers, we were working like clockwork to create policy, develop guidelines, review existing infrastructure, evaluate our prosecution options, and assess the legal framework, while investigating fraud and manipulation, and the dozen other mandates that fell in the agency's lap. The demands were unimaginable but required, and as long as the wheels of bureaucracy churned slowly, they would always be catching up. They are applying old software to a new innovation, operating on a regime created in the 1930s.

The American people and politicians were outraged, and rightfully so. Every agency official, employee, and civil servant he knew, came into work every day dedicated to protecting Americans.

He saw this, gazing out of the office window on the agency floor. Rows and rows of cubicles, staffed with agents bustling, phones ringing, staring at computer screens and their phones, frantically trying to complete their assignments.

He picks up the phone and dials his assistant.

"Patricia, I need you to hold all phone calls. I cannot be disturbed."

"Yes, sir, but you know the National Press has called here five times already requesting a statement on a story they are about to run. And the president is expecting you at two."

"Tell DC Press, the agency has no comment. The National Press can wait for our Press Conference Statement, make sure they are on the list for the stakeholder and press teleconference call as well. And I will be at the White House."

'Click.'

He would be addressing the public and the media soon, and he needed to get his head together.

Was Bitcoin just operating in a bubble, inevitably to burst? Many had compared Bitcoin to the internet age explosion, the dot.com effect. While the perspective of technology insiders was that these virtual currencies could be as powerful as the corporations that created the currency and built their platform structure, if not more.

Blockchain technology powering Bitcoin would reduce the costs of transactions and make access to information flows more efficient. The traditional role of the institution would no longer be needed. A decentralized ecosystem of entities will form together supported by the blockchain technology.

But now panic has ensued. The Bitcoin market plummet that began in the first few days of November were continuing to have a ripple impact in the market. Market insiders had not seen this plummet, but the market volatility, followed by the dramatic and continuous drop in the Bitcoin price from $20,000 to $13,000 to staggering $7,000 precipitated the panic sale. Fluctuations in the market are common, but in a decentralized and destabilized security, there was no owner to turn to as the authoritative source for information, for answers. People have lost hundreds of thousands of dollars, up to millions. The fall in Bitcoin had taken over all the news outlets and social media. Everyone was talking.

Chris begins the walk down the hallway from the department office to the designated press room. He hears the chatter. Officials asking the media to display their media pass badges and verification as journalists. They catch what they believe is a glimpse of him, and all he can hear is "Chairman, I have a question. May I have a moment of your time? What is the SEC position on Bitcoin and market plummet? Is it a security?" as he continues to proceed down the hallway, around the corner to the authorized agency official's access point.

He approaches the podium, outfitted with the U.S. flag and SEC seal. Bright lights are flashing and cameras shuttering. Microphones extended toward him, attached to the arms of reporters starring at him, with their eyes wide open, lips partially open, getting ready to pounce as soon as he finishes his statement.

"I believe in the working men and women of this agency. They come in every day concerned about the investors that are being taken advantage of and those exploited. And the importance of their work is more profound today with the market plummet of Bitcoin. Since the SEC began to apply our regulations to the virtual currency market and virtual instruments, we have informed retail investors to exercise caution and diligence on involvement with entities working in this market for a reason. That reason is that like other markets, but even more so in the virtual currency market, that possesses high levels of instability and volatility, that entities and instruments engaging in investment and trade like behaviors are subject to the SEC regulations. They must be registered with the SEC and comply with the disclosure and reporting requirements. Entities must make it clear to retail investors, to the public, what the risks are in use and investment, the valuation of the company and the basis and metrics for that evaluation, and how the virtual currency, digital asset actually works. Our mandate remains the same today, as it has always been. Prevent fraud and manipulation. Companies know the rules, they have not changed, and they must follow the rules, because we will enforce them."

Fumbling. Whispers.

"Questions?" Chris poses to the media.

"When can the industry expect an assessment by the agency on whether cryptocurrency is a security or not? Will there be a bright line rule issued by the agency?"

Chris answers, "These are complex questions and thus the answer is complex. We must evaluate the structure of the purported cryptocurrency, coin, token, or whatever the label. Labels do not end the inquiry. The assessment of whether there is a security or not is an individual review on a case-by-case basis."

"What has the SEC done or plan to do in light of the Bitcoin market plummet?" Yells a reporter.

"Well, it is not entirely clear to many what happened or did not happen. I can say at this point that we are paying attention and will try to bring clarity to the situation. A formal official investigation has not been launched at the time but if a law was broken, we will do our jobs to enforce the law and protect the American people."

"Chairman, Mr. Donaldson…" states journalist while waving her hand. "Yes, you." Chris points at the woman. The journalist asks, "But without any formal, official guidance, how are entities supposed to know what is allowed and what is not? How can a company function legally, with one hand tied behind their back?"

"I believe I answered that question in my statement. The same rules apply. If it looks like a security investment, future interest, expectation of a return, then quacks like a security, it is a security. This is different and separate from mediums of exchange or stores of value. And if any company ever has a question about their business model, we are more than happy to engage in an open and ongoing dialogue with all stakeholders."

"Chairman Donaldson, is there a reason why you are here, and the CFTC Chairman is not? Wasn't this operation a joint effort between the agencies? Or does the SEC want to take all the credit? When is the CFTC Chairman going to make a statement, or take a position on this? Where is he?"

"I am the SEC Chairman. And I am here. The CFTC Chairman is handling his obligations as chairman now and regrets he is unable to be here today. With that said the Chairman has complete confidence in me that I represent the inter-agency joint task force interests and execute my duties effectively. I wouldn't be in this position if I couldn't do my job."

The journalist follows up, "We notice that your deputy Mitch isn't here either. In fact, he has been missing at quite a few appearances and meetings I am told. I inquire because he is more involved than you in the day-to-day investigation operations for the joint-task force. Would he be available after this to answer any questions?"

Chris responds, "Mitch has done an amazing job and is a crucial member of the SEC and the task force. Joe, the CFTC liaison for the inter-agency task force has worked closely with Mitch as part of our shared commitment to cooperation. He is here and will speak shortly to also answer any questions."

A journalist shouts, "Has the deputy been terminated?! Some say he has also noticeably been missing at the agency, his door is always locked."

Chris interrupts the journalist, "No stirring gossip, it is unbecoming of the press."

Cameras' flash.

A news reporter asks, "But Chairman Donaldson, what do you…"

Chris cuts the reporter off, "Thank you. No further questions."

EPILOGUE

The hearing is postponed and remains in this status for the foreseeable future. At first, it was delayed allowing more time for investigation. The Chairman made it clear that the confidentiality and government secrets privilege prohibited him from discussing most of the investigation in a public hearing. He could prepare a written public statement. The SEC offered to testify in a private hearing to committee members. The public hearing was rescheduled to a private hearing. But a few days before the hearing, the morning newspaper front page headline read, "Inside Job! SEC Chairman Assistant Lead Crypto Ponzi Scheme!"

The media attention forced the Department of Justice to arrest Mitch. Mike wasn't arrested and he wasn't even mentioned by the newspaper. Considering the media attention and newly opened Department of Justice investigation, the

Chairman gave notice to the committee that he was advised by the White House counsel not to testify. The committee members issued a congressional subpoena, but on the day of the hearing, the seat reserved for the Chairman to give testimony was empty. He was sanctioned, and this led to the ongoing legal battle in the courts.

Meanwhile, Bitcoin's future is bright. BC Trusts is doing well. The company manages to come out on the other side of litigation, not unscathed but still standing. African and South American countries are looking at government-backed forms of Bitcoin to bring economic stability. As well as exploring the possibilities blockchain technology can provide for official legal record registration for land, property, and assets. This could help bring transparency, thereby reducing the likelihood of corruption and fraud, which has plagued many countries. Blockchain technology is even being looked to as a potential tool to secure voting and election integrity.

Countries have developed new legal frameworks governing cryptocurrency, such as Japan and Switzerland. Economic development and access to wealth matriculation beyond the wealthy class will improve the standard of living. There is ongoing research to try to leverage the blockchain technology tools, including the public ledger and unique verifiable identifier of transactions, to address inefficiencies in world trade from fragmented trade relationships, quality control issues, theft and fraud, by unifying the transfer of payment, physical goods, and information.

It may have all started out with the premise to cut out the middleman. Banks were screwing people over, taking their life savings, charging fees and high interests' rate of people that are just trying to get by, living paycheck-to-paycheck. Countries are slashing their currency value based on political needs. The people should not have to worry about politics devaluing their currency. That seemed to be at least one motive to only allow a fixed number of Bitcoins in the market. Stabilizing the market's purchasing power free from some self-interest, Bitcoin may not be what Moto and the founders envisioned, neither what he, she, or they intended. But now the people are empowered and know what is possible.

This possibility caught the attention of social media giant LitVibes. They wanted their own currency. Taking advantage of recent criticism that the up and down fluctuations in the value of Bitcoin, social media giant LitVibes publicized their plans to launch a stable coin. The stable coin would be backed by a reserve of assets based on fiat currency and operate on a semi-decentralized financial platform, not a fully decentralized financial platform, different from the Bitcoin, original cryto-currency design. The platform fails to protect anonymity, as the platform would require identification to be verified.

Forget sending messages and liking pictures, they want to control your money and financial transactions too. Control of your data is not enough for them. Alarms should have been ringing because it does not make sense to trust them with more of your information and money. LitVibes has been embroiled in scandal from verified reports and leaks proving rampant misuse, abuse, and data privacy breaches. Not to mention LitVibes has amassed a powerhouse in a little over ten years through monetization of people's data. Yes, they got rich off the people and continue to do so, and the people did not get a dime. Their power and international reach is immeasurable because of their billions of account holders, where just by means of scale, they aim to influence the global value of currency. LitVibes could control and power the market, ultimately controlling the people more and more. And this is not unfathomable, where LitVibes is interwoven into nearly every daily action of our lives, serves as a substitute for real life social interactions, and refuge for self-validation. But the people have a choice on who controls the market and who powers the market. Hopefully, they choose wisely and make their voices heard. Moto is depending on them.

The legality of the various off shoots of Bitcoin among other types of innovative digital assets is up in the air. But the government is watching. Most hope to be classified as a commodity, subject to CFTC regulation, and try to avoid classification as a security, so that they are not subject to the SEC registration. The SEC has strict requirements on custody and safekeeping of investor assets, valuation, disclosures regarding the complexities of the products and technology, and the risks of price volatility, plus state-by-state regulations. However, there is no clear guidance on what classifies as a security or not. Rather, there is a patchwork of opinions and settlement decrees that best serve as examples of how the SEC can treat a digital asset that seems like an investment and is set up in a similar manner to the digital asset involved in that particular case example.

So far only one major digital token has been classified as currency and received a hefty fine of $700,000 for selling a virtual currency without being unregistered with FinCen, although most cryptocurrencies operate as a medium of exchange. Classification as a property operates as more of an assessment of whether the owner of the digital asset earned a profit, taxable income that must be reported to the IRS. The diversity in the digital asset field is the beauty of the innovation of crypto. No one wants to be the same because they want a unique market share that will allow them to achieve success and longevity. But at the same time, they may not want to be too different in technical aspects, as the more different, the more complex the assessment for classification and the more risk for liability. This is what happens when cryptocurrency becomes a business.

At the core, Bitcoin allowed for two people to transact directly with each other without going through a third party. Bitcoin, a series of ones and zeros, successfully shook-up the financial market system and that was the point.

ACKNOWLEDGEMENTS

——

Foremost, I will like to acknowledge all my family, friends, and colleagues, who have been my biggest supporters on this journey. I must thank my mother Michelle and her husband Manning, my siblings Michael, Kyana, Sam, Autumn, and Bianca, my Aunt Val and Uncle Speedy, my cousin Ariel, Laura, Ms. Usher, Santa and Pedro for their unwavering support all my life. I will also like to recognize my best friends Aaron, Amber, Andria, Khadija, Lamar, Lee, Michelle, Tawanna, Tovah, Yone and my sorority sisters.

I am grateful for all those who took the time to let me interview them for my novel. The insights and expertise of these individuals are invaluable and strengthen my commitment to civil liberties and the use of technology to serve communities of color.

Renee Aggarwal, PhD. *(Vice Provost for Faculty, McDonough Professor of Finance & Director, Center for Financial Markets & Policy, Georgetown University)*

Christopher Brummer, Esq. *(Agnes N. Williams Research Professor & Faculty Director of Institute of International Economic Law, Georgetown University Law Center)*

Alex Gladstein *(Chief Strategy Officer, Human Rights Foundation)*

Donna Redel, MBA *(CEO & Founder, Strategic 50; Professor at Fordham University School of Law)*

Patrick McCarty, Esq. *(Founder & President, McCarty Financial, LLC)*

Patrick Murck, Esq. *(Affiliate, Berkman Klein Center for Internet & Society at Harvard University)*

Words cannot express my appreciation to New Degree Press and the team of editors for their patience, professional advice and assistance. I am glad I took you up on the challenge to become a published author!